GOING THE
SECOND
MILE

MEL BLACKABY

Multnomah® Publishers *Sisters, Oregon*

GOING THE SECOND MILE
published by Multnomah Publishers, Inc.

© 2006 by Melvin D. Blackaby
International Standard Book Number: 1-59052-515-9

Cover design by The DesignWorks Group, Inc.
Cover image by Veer, Inc.

Unless otherwise indicated, Scripture quotations are from:
The Holy Bible, New King James Version
© 1984 by Thomas Nelson, Inc.
Other Scripture quotations are from:
New American Standard Bible © (NASB) © 1960, 1977, 1995
by the Lockman Foundation. Used by permission.
Holman Christian Standard Bible (HCSB)
Copyright © 1999, 2000, 2002, 2003 by Holman Bible Publishers,
Nashville Tennessee. All rights reserved.
The Holy Bible, New International Version (NIV)
© 1973, 1984 by International Bible Society,
used by permission of Zondervan Publishing House

Multnomah is a trademark of Multnomah Publishers, Inc.,
and is registered in the U.S. Patent and Trademark Office.
The colophon is a trademark of Multnomah Publishers, Inc.

For information:
MULTNOMAH PUBLISHERS, INC. • 601 NORTH LARCH STREET • SISTERS, OREGON 97759

Library of Congress Cataloging-in-Publication Data
Blackaby, Melvin D.
Going the second mile / Mel Blackaby.
p. cm.
ISBN 1-59052-515-9
1. Christian life. 2. Self-denial. I. Title.
BV4647.S4B53 2006
248.4—dc22
2006015637

06 07 08 09 10 11—10 9 8 7 6 5 4 3 2 1 0

To Gina,
who has gone the second mile with me
from the day we were married

CONTENTS

FOR YOUR JOY

By Henry T. Blackaby

The greatest privilege of a parent is to see their children choose to walk with the "God of their father." It has been my privilege not only to witness that in my son's life, but also to serve the Lord with him as we travel and speak together at conferences all over the world.

Mel has written this book out of his own life experiences. Even as a boy I watched the Lord's hand upon him as he responded to what the Lord was doing in his life. As a teenager and then a college student he was called upon to "go the second mile," to go beyond what was acceptable to those around him. These moments were choices he had to make even when those around him refused to go that way.

As Mel serves now as a pastor, the Lord has developed his character with a true "shepherd's heart." The shepherd is often called upon to carry burdens many others will not carry, spending extra long hours with hurting and bewildered people. But I have sensed that Mel, in the midst of carrying the burdens of God's people, has discovered a level of joy that is found only in a genuine relationship with Jesus Christ. While others are burning out, he has grown stronger. And by his example he is leading many of God's people to experience the joy of going the second mile with their Lord.

This book is Mel's witness to the reality of abundant life in Christ. You will be drawn to this experience for yourself as you read and as you identify the Lord's activity in your life.

There is so much more to the Christian life than many people are experiencing. When Christ said He came to bring abundant life, He really did mean it. As you read this book, may you hear the Lord's invitation to go the second mile with Him and experience life as He intended when He created you.

YOU HAVE ONLY ONE LIFE

Make It More Than Just Good

The world today is desperate to find God. Many people are searching for Him. But when they look at those who claim to be Christians, I wonder if they see the good news of Christ and are drawn to Him.

As I observe people, I'm convinced that there's a restlessness in their souls…though many can't put their finger on it. They don't know what's missing. And when they look to the church and to those who call themselves Christians, they see no real difference between what they observe and the life they already have.

One of the great hindrances faced by people who are examining the Christian faith is actually Christians themselves. Not that Christians aren't good people; they are! But the world doesn't need to see good people doing good things for their God; they need to see *God* within them, doing what only *He* can do!

When it comes down to it, there are a lot of good people in the world. There are many wonderful things people do and many great causes they support. There are many talented individuals who use their gifts for noble and charitable purposes. In many cases, the lives of those who don't know Christ look even better than the lives of those who claim to be Christians.

Should there be a difference between a good person and a child of God? Absolutely. Christians are not called to be merely good people; God is after something much more than that. He's after something that cannot be accomplished without His presence; something that goes beyond what a good person is able to do. It's what I call *living your life on the second mile*. The world will respect a good deed, but will marvel at those who walk with the Lord on the second mile.

However, I've known many Christians who work hard for the Lord and yet are still struggling, and whose spirits are troubled. They tend to strive ever harder in hopes of gaining a blessing or earning a reward from God. And the more they strive the more frustrated they get. They actually burn out trying to do good things in the name of the Lord!

If that describes your life, you need to understand the second mile. For going the second mile is not a more hectic or burdensome life; it is much more peaceful. Better yet, it is full of the adventure of walking with Christ into places even a good person would not go.

You have one life to live, so live it well. Live it as God intended…and make a difference for eternity.

May the Holy Spirit open your eyes to see your life from God's perspective and give you the courage to adjust to Him.

* * *

Note: At times throughout this book, people's names have been changed to protect their privacy.

A WORD OF ACKNOWLEDGMENT

No pastor can tell the stories of God without acknowledging the church family that walks with him. Together our church has seen God do many mighty acts in our midst, and it's all because I serve among a congregation willing to walk by faith and follow the Lord. So I say thank you to Bow Valley Baptist Church, whose members demonstrate a significant measure of faith, sacrifice, and grace.

A special thanks to our pastoral team, Bo, Jonathan, Jeremy, and Lynn, who with such joy carry a load most people would never understand. And to Margy, my faithful assistant, who keeps everything going smoothly…usually.

To God be the glory!

CHAPTER ONE

THE ROAD LESS TRAVELED

Seeing Our Need

For the love of Christ compels us...
2 Corinthians 5:14

E ver had one of those days when you don't feel appreciated for all the good things you do?

It was a Sunday of all days when I hit that wall the hardest.

I was a university student trying my best to live a good Christian life. But I kept running into people who took advantage of my kindness and wanted my help. Nobody seemed to care about *me,* but only about what I could do for them.

I was feeling lonely and unappreciated. I went to church that night, and it happened again: "Mel, my car broke down on the highway; I need your help to fix it." So as a good Christian, I did my duty and said, "Sure."

Only then did I discover that the car was forty-five minutes away. And as I pulled out of the church parking lot, the cold rain that had been falling all day began turning to sleet.

The only bright spot in all this was an attractive young girl who wanted to go with us. She was new to the church and on my "prospect list." So I put on a good face as I sped off to help a friend in need.

LOW AND ALONE

We came to the abandoned car on the side of the highway. I knew this wasn't going to be fun, but we grabbed our tools and got to work. We had to slide under the car, which was parked over a puddle, so in no time we were cold, wet, and feeling downright miserable.

Soon my friend couldn't take it any longer and wanted to call it quits. But there was no way I was going out there again the next day, so I forged on while he went back to my car to warm up…with the girl. I had one of those strange feelings—cold on the outside, burning up on the inside. But I pushed ahead and eventually had the car ready to drive.

As I stumbled back to my nice warm car, I heard the sound of giggling. The two of them were having the time of their lives, obviously unconcerned about how I was doing. But at least the good deed was over and I could enjoy a leisurely drive back with the young lady—so I thought. When my friend went to his car, she went with him!

I stared in unbelief as their car pulled onto the highway and drove off. But it was true: I was all alone.

On my way back I was feeling pretty low. Absorbed in self-pity, I missed a critical exit and headed over a bridge that took me a long way from where I needed to be. It would take me an extra twenty minutes to reach home. By this time I was frustrated as well as feeling hurt and lonesome.

I was frustrated as well as feeling hurt and lonesome.

At my lowest point, I remember welling up with emotion. At that moment I heard the Lord speak. Though I was all alone, His presence was clear and unmistakable—so much that I literally turned and looked at the passenger seat, expecting to see Him sitting there. Though I saw no physical form, my spirit heard him say, "Mel…"

"Yes, Lord," I responded.

"Stop whining!"

I thought to myself, *Now that's a little insensitive! Lord, I'm having a moment here.*

But soon I began to understand. It was as if the Lord was saying, "Now you know how *I* feel. The only time we talk is when you need something. The only time we spend together is when you're desperate for My help. And worst of all, *you've forgotten how much I've done for you.*"

I began reflecting on what God had done in my life, how blessed I was, how loved I was. If all I'd received from Him was salvation, that would be far more than I deserved; but God hadn't stopped there—He had shown me grace beyond measure.

The more I reflected on this, the more my spirit lifted and my sorrow turned to joy. He brought to mind events that had shaped my life, people who had invested in me, and so many good things I'd experienced. It was as though my life flashed before my eyes and I saw His hand in every stage.

His presence throughout my life was obvious. And my awareness of this seemed to make everything all right as I continued home that night.

COMPELLED BY LOVE

After all God had done in my life, how could I complain about helping others in need? I was ashamed as I thought more about my previous attitude.

I also came to realize that my service to others had been motivated by recognition I hoped to receive from them—not by love for God and appreciation for His love and blessings for me.

✦ True Christianity is a life compelled by the love of Christ—
nothing more, nothing less. The apostle Paul understood this
when he wrote, "For Christ's love compels us, since we have
reached this conclusion: If One died for all, then all died. And
He died for all so that those who live should no longer live for
themselves, but for the One who died for them and was raised"
(2 Corinthians 5:14–15, HCSB).

How fully do you realize that everything God has done
for you, He did not *have* to do? He has chosen to act toward
you in a way that's totally foreign to our way of thinking—His
thoughts are not our thoughts, and His ways are not our ways
(Isaiah 55:8–9). God does things that human beings would
never do: He shows mercy to sinners; He forgives their sin and
cleanses their lives (think of it: "While we were yet sinners,
Christ died for us"!—Romans 5:8, NASB); He protects them
from all evil, supplies their every need with good things, and
grants them eternal life in heaven. Yet He doesn't have to do
any of this.

Oh, the wonder of God's great salvation! The person who
understands it will be changed forever. To those who repent of
their sin and put their faith in Jesus Christ, God shows mercy
and grace—He withholds that which we rightfully deserve as
sinners and pours out blessings we don't deserve.

In light of what God has done in our lives, we ought to
live worthy of the gospel of Jesus Christ, and worthy of His
sacrifice.

THE SMILE OF CHRIST

I've generally considered myself to be sacrificial, ready to do whatever it takes to follow the Lord. My understanding of sacrifice, however, took on a much deeper meaning when I joined a group from our church that went to Mozambique on a mission trip.

I'd been on several short-term mission projects within North America and had given lots of money so others could go on missions, but this was the first foreign mission trip I'd really experienced for myself. Because of it, I'll never be the same.

I met a man in Mozambique named Lavish. He was the pastor of a small church in the capital city, but he also had a mission church in a small fishing village on the Indian Ocean. We were excited to go out to this remote area where there had been no church whatsoever. A year earlier, we had sent a team there to secure some land on which we could build a church. Our job was now to do construction work on the church building with the village men, have a Bible study with the women, do various sports activities among the children, drill a water well for the village, and show the *Jesus* film for the entire community.

Everyone on the team was prepared for their assignment and ready for some long, hard days. We were tired of talking about sacrifice in our comfortable church back home; we were ready to put action to our words.

At that remote village, we slept in tents, cooked over an open fire, and constructed a bathroom with no more than a shovel. (You get the picture!) Ministry among the people was great. Many responded to Christ, and I had the opportunity to conduct a baptism in the Crocodile River (another story in itself).

Meanwhile, with great interest I watched Lavish as he worked alongside us. It was evident to all that he was living the abundant life Christ had promised. His smile would grab you and pull you in, and I couldn't remember meeting anyone so full of the joy of the Lord.

It was evident to all that he was living the abundant life Christ promised.

SACRIFICE

As our time of ministry came to an end, we decided to give away our tents, cooking equipment, and extra clothes. Not wanting to create a riot in the village, we decided to take all these goods to the pastor's house in the capital city, where he could distribute them as he saw fit.

We loaded the items into a truck and drove across the city to Lavish's house, a place we had not yet seen. He led us through a section of town where we would have never gone alone. I couldn't believe my eyes! I'd never seen such poverty and dire living conditions. It was worse than any ghetto I could imagine.

It was getting dark as we drove down narrow dirt roads lined with shelters made of salvaged rubbish. I was captured by the sight of people wandering in the night, just as they were no doubt intrigued to see foreigners driving into their neighborhood.

When the truck came to a stop, we jumped out. I quickly loaded up Lavish with some of the goods, then went to grab some myself. When I turned around, however, he was gone.

My eyes darted around, trying to figure out where Lavish lived, but I saw nothing that made sense. As I started walking in the direction I thought he'd gone, I caught a glimpse of him turning into a tavern. I looked in the tavern door just in time to see Lavish going out the back door. I quickly started through this local hangout, trying to appear confident in what appeared to be a very dangerous place. I walked as tall as possible, flexed a few muscles, and did my best to look like a guy you didn't want to mess with! Everyone inside stared at the white boy with his arms full of articles they would love to have for themselves.

Before anyone inside could react, I made it out the back door and into a small dirt courtyard. At the other end was something like a cement box with a metal door. There stood Lavish, unlocking the padlock to let me into his home.

We stepped into a room almost empty. Just a cot, a few rustic cooking utensils, a small stack of clothes, and a single lightbulb hanging from the ceiling. I surveyed the room, trying not to look as if I were checking out his house. I was stunned to realize there was no running water or bathroom to be seen.

When my eyes returned to Lavish, I was struck by the radiance of his smile. Then he said something that cut me to the heart: "Thank you so much for helping us; your sacrifice has been great."

Sacrifice? I felt ashamed, knowing that what I held in my hands cost more than he owned. As I stood in the home of a fellow pastor and thought of all I enjoy at home, how could I consider my service a sacrifice? It was Lavish who had made the ultimate sacrifice for the Lord. He had a good job at the airport, but gave all his income to support his church and its mission. Moreover, he spoke six different languages and had the skills to pursue a much more lucrative job if he wanted to devote his time to it. But he considered his calling as a pastor to be the greatest privilege in the world.

In the world's eyes, he had nothing. But as far as Lavish was concerned, he had everything. You could tell it by the look in his eyes. He knew the Lord, and the joy of the Lord was bubbling out of his life.

Lavish had found the Lord…on the second mile. And nothing else mattered.

Let's find out more of what this "second mile" is all about in the life that God has called *each* of us to.

CHAPTER TWO

BEYOND DUTY

Seeing God's Love

And whoever compels you to go one mile, go with him two.
Matthew 5:41

Take a close look at a passage of Scripture that may be quite disturbing the more you truly reflect on it. Here Jesus commands a kind of conduct that goes against every natural response we have and sets a standard that can seem so unfair:

🍃 You have heard that it was said, "An eye for an eye and a tooth for a tooth." But I tell you not to resist an evil person. But whoever slaps you on your right cheek, turn the other to him also. If anyone wants to sue you and take away your tunic, let him have your cloak also. And whoever compels you to go one mile, go with him two. Give to him who asks you, and from him who wants to borrow from you do not turn away.

You have heard that it was said, "You shall love your neighbor and hate your enemy." But I say to you, love your enemies, bless those who curse you, do good to those who hate you, and pray for those who spitefully use you and persecute you, that you may be sons of your Father in heaven; for He makes His sun rise on the evil and on the good, and sends rain on the just and on the unjust. (Matthew 5:38–45)

If ever there was a passage the world cannot understand—and that the Christian *must* understand—this is it.

 If ever there was a passage the Christian must understand, this is it.

A FAMILIAR PICTURE

The second mile is the road Jesus has called us to walk, and this is where you'll find Him doing His work.

This image of the second mile comes from a situation that every Jew in Jesus' day was familiar with. It refers to the Roman law requiring any person, when asked, to carry a Roman soldier's pack for one mile. As soldiers would travel through the land, they carried all their belongings with them. To relieve the load, they would conscript someone to carry their pack. But at the end of one mile, that person could, by law, drop the pack and walk away. One mile was the limit of their duty. At that point, the soldier would either have to carry it himself or recruit another person to take it the next mile.

As you can imagine, carrying the load wasn't the worst part of the task. The Jews had always been proud; after all, they were God's chosen people. Roman soldiers meanwhile were part of a foreign government that had forcefully occupied their land. To be required to aid the enemy was both humiliating and downright infuriating to a Jew. And yet Jesus said, "Whoever compels you to go one mile, go with him two."

How would you respond to such a statement? "You've got to be kidding! They're the *enemy!* I don't want to carry a soldier's pack for the required one mile, let alone voluntarily take it for another."

That's exactly why Jesus asks us to go the second mile. It's beyond what those around us have a right to expect from us…but *not* beyond what Jesus does, or asks us to do.

Jesus wasn't telling us, "Do your duty." He was really saying, "Do what is *not* your duty." It isn't your duty to go the second mile, turn the other cheek, or give beyond what's expected. But Jesus said His disciples should always impart grace—to show far more good toward others than is deserved. They'll do the unexpected, go much further than required, and do that which is beyond reasonable expectation. Why? Not because the recipient deserves it, but because we remember that we didn't deserve the grace shown to us when Jesus saved us.

As difficult to hear as those "second-mile" words must have been for His disciples, Jesus went even further. In case anyone misunderstood His imagery of the second mile, Jesus made His point clear: "Love your enemies, bless those who curse you, do good to those who hate you, and pray for those who spitefully use you and persecute you" (Matthew 5:44). Why?

In the next verse, Jesus gives the reason: "That you may be sons of your Father in heaven." This is what demonstrates the difference Christ makes in your life when you're born again and receive the gift of the Holy Spirit. After all, everybody loves those who love them in return; that's natural for the entire human race. But to love those who hate you—that's supernatural. It's evidence of the divine nature within your mortal body (see 2 Peter 1:4).

This is what demonstrates the difference Christ makes in your life.

And the only way to get there is to walk the second mile with Jesus.

The sad reality, however, is that many Christians want a "second helping" not the "second mile." We want the promise of abundant life, but we define such a life by the world's standard. We instinctively strive for a life of ease and want to take the path of least resistance, doing the minimum of service to others required by "duty," but nothing more. That's naturally what all people want; that's life on the first mile. And it takes us away from the place God wants us to be, the place where He is at work...

FROM THE HEART

When it comes to serving God, have you ever seen someone do the right thing for the wrong reasons?

When I read the Bible, it speaks more about attitudes of the heart than it does activity. In fact, in God's eyes, you can do the right thing and still be wrong.

Consider the people Jesus watched one day who were putting money into the temple treasury (Mark 12:41–44). The passage notes that "many who were rich put in much." They not only gave to the Lord's work; they gave *lots*. Could anything be better than that?

Jesus, however, looked deeper. He noted that "all" these rich persons "put in out of their abundance." But there was also a poor widow woman who put in only "two mites," yet truly gave sacrificially: "She out of her poverty put in all that she had, her whole livelihood," Jesus observed.

Those two widow's mites represented a heart that loved God and a faith that trusted His provision. Jesus declared that "this poor widow has put in more than all those who have given to the treasury" (v. 43), although the others gave far more money. Jesus saw the difference between genuine love and religious activity. He saw what really mattered from God's perspective—a pure heart. Jesus wasn't trying to get people to *act right*, but to *be right*. He wanted to show the difference between service that emerges from the heart and service driven by duty.

No, it isn't our *duty* to go the second mile, but that's what makes the Christian stand out from the world.

 No, it isn't your DUTY to go the second mile—but that's what makes a Christian stand out from the world.

Gratefully Sharing Our Blessings

I like to experience food from various parts of the world. As a result of my travels, I've come to enjoy a special kind of dough-nut that's unavailable where I live in Canada.

On one occasion, someone in our church was on a busi-ness trip to Houston, Texas, and brought back with him six dozen of my favorite doughnuts—some to keep and some to give to friends. I remember how my mouth instantaneously began to water when he came to my office and hand-delivered a dozen of those doughnuts. It was a good day.

But there was a problem: Word leaked out. And I have friends who have the same weakness I have.

To share, or not to share—that was the question. As a pastor, I knew I needed to set a good example. So I thought to myself, *Perhaps I could tithe my doughnuts and give 1.2 away.* But I realized that wouldn't work.

Then I thought, *What would Jesus do?* I surmised that He would probably bless the doughnuts, multiply them, and feed them to five thousand people. So I tried that—but still had only twelve.

In the midst of my dilemma, I had a growing internal conviction. I couldn't get the thought out of my mind: *"Someone else* paid for the doughnuts; I didn't. *He* carried them all the way from Houston; I didn't. *He* was generous and self-sacrificing in offering them to others, yet I'm still struggling to share something I received as a gift."

The fact is that my friend's generosity became my motivation. I realized that when you receive a great blessing, you can't turn around and hoard it for yourself. To whom much is given, much is required. "For everyone to whom much is given, from him much will be required" (Luke 12:48).

So I shared those doughnuts.

THE DRIVING FORCE

Do you understand how generous God has been toward you? Are you thankful for it?

• The driving force that motivates us on the second mile is a thankful heart. The second mile is our response to the love of Christ. That's what compels us. That's what drives us.

Once we come to know the heart of God, it forever changes our life. We experience the love of God reaching out to us while we were yet sinners. We receive the mercy of God that withheld punishment due us because of sin. We know the grace of God that has freely given us what we don't deserve. We're set free from our past life and given hope of a future with God. We enjoy the kindness flowing from the generous heart of God pouring blessing into our life.

God then expects us to live our lives as a reflection of our grateful understanding of what we've received from Him.

The second mile is a reflection of our thankfulness for the love of Christ in our life.

• Any good person can walk the first mile, but the second mile is a reflection of the love of Christ in our life and of our thankfulness for it. Only those who have truly experienced the love of Christ—and are truly grateful—are capable of passing it on.

Knowing how much God has done in your own life, how have you received it? How much have you given back to Him?

Throughout the Bible

The Bible is full of commands to live life on the second mile, commands that describe the character of the Christian life—as well as passages that illustrate the difference.

Consider again, for example, the Lord's words in Matthew 5:43–45. Here we see the first mile:

> You have heard that it was said, "You shall love your neighbor and hate your enemy."

And also the second:

> But I say to you, love your enemies, bless those who curse you, do good to those who hate you, and pray for those who spitefully use you and persecute you, that you may be sons of your Father in heaven.

Or take the apostle Paul's words in Philippians 2:4. Again we see the first mile:

> Let each of you look out not only for his own interests...

And it's followed by the second:

> ...but also for the interests of others.

The priest and the Levite on the Jericho Road went the first mile when they let nothing interrupt their journey toward their scheduled business; the good Samaritan was going the second mile when he stopped to thoroughly assist the wounded traveler whom the priest and Levite had stepped around (Luke 10:30–35).

We glimpse first-mile thinking in the large numbers of those who followed Jesus in the early part of His ministry; we find a second-mile perspective only in the much smaller group who affirmed, "Lord…You have the words of eternal life." They stayed with Jesus even when "many of His disciples went back and walked with Him no more" after recognizing that His teaching on discipleship was "a hard saying" (John 6:60–68).

In Paul's words to the Thessalonian believers, we observe the first mile when Paul speaks of how he and his fellow workers were "well pleased" to share with them the good news of salvation; we look beyond to the second mile when Paul says that they imparted "not only the gospel of God, *but also our own lives*" in "laboring night and day" (1 Thessalonians 2:8–9).

We read how the Macedonian believers went the first mile in supporting the Lord's work financially, as they gave "according to their ability"; these same believers went the second mile when, according to Paul's further commendation, they actually gave *"beyond* their ability" (2 Corinthians 8:3).

Consider what the Lord is trying to say to you through

each of these passages, as well as in other verses you'll find throughout Scripture that reveal the difference between the first and the second mile.

THE VIEW FROM THE SECOND MILE: SEEING GOD'S LOVE

The difference between the first mile and the second mile is a million miles apart.

On the second mile, you're no longer alone.

On the first mile, you can stand on your own. You're doing what any good person would do. Your reward is the applause of people and the satisfaction of a job well done. You see what *you* could accomplish—but nothing more.

The second mile looks much different. You're no longer alone, but you take your stand with Christ. You demonstrate that you're more than a good person; you're a child of God. As a result, people see something different in you—the love of God. For the God of love is now doing His work in you, and the world sees Him.

The difference is clear: The world sees *us* on the first mile; they see *Christ* on the second.

When you walk with Christ on the second mile, people will notice. They may not be able to explain it, but they'll see a qualitative difference in your life.

What are people seeing in your life? Do they see a good person? Or do they see the love of God?

CHAPTER THREE

MORE THAN A GOOD PERSON

Seeing God's Purpose

...conformed to the image of His Son...
Romans 8:29

Darin and Glen were new to our community and bought a house right next to a family in our church. It was more than fate—God wanted to express His love to them through the lives of Herb and Kathy.

Darin looked out his window on a cold winter morning to see his neighbor shoveling snow off his sidewalk. When his wife told him to go out and help, he replied, "Why? He seems to be doing a great job!"

Darin and Glen had known good neighbors before, but nothing like this. And the kindness continued in so many ways.

SECOND-MILE NEIGHBORS

Herb just kept going above and beyond what was expected of a good neighbor. After cutting his grass, his lawn mower would just naturally find its way over to cut Darin's grass. He helped Darin put up a fence and build a shed, gave a hand to renovate their basement, cared for the house when Darin and Glen were out of town, and did anything he could do to lend a hand.

 They were constantly finding ways to show the love of Christ.

Kathy was the same, constantly finding ways to show the love of Christ. They would often share a meal, and the friendship continued to grow.

The day came when Herb and Kathy told them they were moving to a new house, and they couldn't imagine life without their neighbors. At that moment Darin and Glen realized they had really come to love their "Christian friends." Since they were still in the same community, the two couples remained close and their friendship continued to grow.

One day, Kathy invited Glen to go with her to a Bible study at church. How could she refuse? She'd come to love Kathy and trusted her completely. But it was all so new, because to this point church had never been a part of Glen's life.

The more she went to church, however, the more bitter Darin became—not at Herb and Kathy, but at Glen for spending more and more time at the church. But she couldn't help it; something inside her said, "This is right." So she started attending worship services and got to know more and more people at the church.

Then came the day Darin got a call that his dad, who lived in a distant city, had suffered a heart attack. He was in critical condition in a hospital and was to have quadruple bypass surgery. The news hit Darin hard; he felt disoriented, helpless to know what to do. Life suddenly took on new meaning as he considered the possibility of losing his father.

Then Glen came home from church with a bewildered look on her face. She told her husband, "You wouldn't believe what happened at church. In the morning service, the pastor stopped and asked the whole church to pray for your dad!"

Darin couldn't believe it. "Why would all those people pray for my dad when they don't even know him?"

When Darin flew out to be with his father, he discovered that a pastor had been contacted and had already been to the hospital to see his dad. Darin no longer felt alone and helpless, for there was a church family walking with him. His dad made a remarkable recovery, and Darin made a significant discovery: There is a God who loves him.

It wasn't long before Glen gave her life to Christ and was radically changed. Darin couldn't deny that something had happened to his wife. Although he didn't fully understand it, he liked it.

He came to church to see her baptized and decided right

then he had to find out what this Christianity thing was all about.

He began to realize what motivated his neighbors to love him so much.

As he learned more of how much God had done for him, he began to realize what motivated his neighbors to love him so much. Darin, too, gave his life to Christ and was baptized into the church that had gone the second mile for him.

Why did Darin and Glen come to Christ? Because they saw Christ in their neighbors. And once they saw Christ, they fell in love with Him.

Today, Darin and Glen serve as deacons in our church. And they, too, live on the second mile, giving themselves away as some of the most generous and kind people in our church.

BEYOND GOOD

People respect a good person, but good people are not what God has called us to be. He's after something much more than that. He's after something supernatural. He's after something we cannot be in our own strength. He wants to demonstrate the difference between a good person and a child of God.

It is not good people who go to heaven, but only those

who do the will of the heavenly Father (see Matthew 7:21). Furthermore, the Father's will is not something we discover on our own, but is revealed only through a relationship with Jesus Christ (Luke 10:22). Moreover, that which the Father asks us to do will usually make no sense to human reasoning—as is true in the "second mile" passage we looked at earlier.

Striving to be a good person is a noble pursuit but is none-theless of no eternal value. What *is* of eternal value—and what we're called to—is an obedient relationship to Christ whereby He is Lord, and whereby He displays His own life through us.

Goodness is a quality attainable by people on their own; Christlikeness requires divine intervention. Going the second mile is beyond what a good person would do...but not beyond what Jesus does. His measure of goodness far outstrips what the world even deems possible.

The World Sees Christ

Going the second mile, as Jesus describes it in Matthew 5:41, is something that reveals the humility of being a Christian. I guarantee you this: You cannot imitate the nature of Christ. It's either in you or it isn't.

The second mile has been established by Jesus Christ; *His* goodness is our standard and our model. *His* attitude toward us ought to be reflected in our treatment of other people. In other words, *we* must walk as *He* walked.

But no amount of determination can sustain a Christlike attitude over the long haul. In fact, the more you come to understand the life God has called us to live, the more you realize how impossible such a life is in our own strength. That's why God must conform us to the image of Christ (Romans 8:29).

No amount of determination can sustain a Christlike attitude over the long haul.

If your heart has been indwelt by the person of Jesus Christ, others will see Christ. If your heart has been shaped only by the world, the best the world can see in you is a good person.

Jesus doesn't want you to reflect the world; He wants you to reflect the manner in which God has loved you. Love people, help them, and be kind to them. Show mercy, just as your Father showed you mercy. And remember that the way in which you measure your kindness to others, your heavenly Father will measure back to you.

The difference between Christ's way and the world's way is obvious. In the world, if a person doesn't hit back, he's a coward. But to God, it's evidence that Jesus is living in that person's heart. This kind of action isn't a case of being self-controlled, but Christ-controlled.

In the world's way, if a person insults you, your defenses immediately go up. But for the Christian, a personal insult becomes an opportunity to reveal the incredible sweetness of Christ in our life.

The result of our showing such grace toward others is that the world sees Christ in us. The world will respect a good deed...but will marvel at the love of God expressed on the second mile.

People usually don't remember it later when they're told about God's love, but they never forget when they *experience* God's love. The clear mark of a Christian is doing the unexpected, doing what isn't normal for the world to do. Not seeking to be like the world, the one who has been born again will naturally stand out because he or she is different...reflecting the nature of God.

This is what the Lord was talking about when He said, "Let your light so shine before men, that they may see your good works and *glorify your Father who is in heaven*" (Matthew 5:16). The second mile—that's where the Christian life begins.

FIGHTING EVIL WITH GOOD

This passage on the second mile is in the middle of the Sermon on the Mount, and throughout the sermon, Jesus is talking about the character of a Christian. He challenges us not to follow the rigid letter of the law as a means to please God, but to live according to the spirit of the Law. We're to give priority to eternal things and live life accordingly.

Never forget that the world is lost and going to hell, and only Christ can save them. They don't need to see a good person; they need to see *Christ in us*. So don't fight with an evil person. If he treats you wrongly…big deal! You don't forget that God treats you pretty well. If an evil person insults you… who cares what he thinks? You don't forget that God loves you. If an evil person wants to take your shirt…give him a coat too. If he makes you go one mile…go two miles, and blow him away. Fight evil with good. Don't make the evil person the measure of your response; make God the measure of your response. And God's measure is that He never lowers Himself to the level of sinful action or words.

Make God the measure of your response.

In every area of your life, be generous when you don't have to be. In relationships, forgive freely, show kindness, and be gentle. At work, give your best, do more than is expected, and live with integrity. In service to God's people, give generously, serve willingly, and lay down your life for the sake of the Lord. *Go the second mile!*

Let me say it once more: The world sees *us* on the first mile; they see *Christ* on the second.

ONLY GETTING BY?

Dietrich Bonhoeffer coined the term *cheap grace*, a reference to taking the grace of God lightly. Some people have the attitude, "If God can forgive anything I do, then I can do anything I like. All I have to do is come back and ask forgiveness, and He'll gladly forgive me, because He's a God of love." Don't count on it! Yes, God can forgive any sin, but that doesn't mean He will. Repentance is required. Unless there is godly sorrow leading to repentance and a changed life, sin remains.

But there's another attitude among Christians that's equally disturbing. I'm referring to those who seek to do the minimum requirement as Christians, those who simply want to get by and be ensured of a home in heaven. In the Christian life, there's no such thing as the minimum. It's all or nothing.

That was the example the apostle Paul has given us in how he responded to God's grace. Paul wrote,

> For I am the least of the apostles, and not fit to be called an apostle, because I persecuted the church of God. But by the grace of God I am what I am, and His grace toward me did not prove vain; but I labored even more than all of them, yet not I, but the grace of God with me. (1 Corinthians 15:9–10, NASB)

Now that we've been forgiven of our sin and are in the family of God, we should not remain in sin. Now that we're in the family of God, we should not be asking, "What's the minimum requirement of God? What's the least I can do for Him and still get into heaven?" Rather we should say, "Lord, I give my all to You." Knowing what God has done for us, how can we have the audacity to slight Him with a casual attitude? He is our *life!* Apart from Him we have nothing!

From a Right Heart

Give the Lord your all, remembering that He said, "Give, and it will be given to you: good measure, pressed down, shaken together, and running over will be put into your bosom. For with the same measure that you use, it will be measured back to you" (Luke 6:38). Remember also that the One who measures what comes back to you is God, not the world.

We don't give so we can get something back; and yet, no one can outgive God. When you give your life to serve Him, He just pours a blessing right back into your life. It's a kingdom principle: You try to save your life, you'll lose it. But if you give your life away for His sake, you'll find it (Matthew 16:25).

 God doesn't reward your duty; He rewards your heart.

But you must understand this: In urging you to give your all, I'm not talking about more work or giving great gifts to God. If you give a great deal of money to the church, or work your fingers to the bone for the Lord, yet still find abundant life elusive—remember that God is reading the heart from which you serve. He doesn't reward your duty; He rewards your heart.

I sometimes hear people say, "I'll do it, but I won't like it." I want to immediately cry out, "Then drop to your knees and get your heart right!" Admitting you have a bad attitude doesn't make that attitude acceptable to God. Hard work doesn't compensate for a hard heart. Repenting from your bad attitude is the only thing pleasing to God. And when you do repent, He'll forgive your sin, cleanse your life, and fill you with the joy of serving Him.

The Bible tells us, "The eyes of the LORD run to and fro throughout the whole earth, to show Himself strong on behalf of those whose heart is loyal to Him" (2 Chronicles 16:9). When your heart is wholly committed to God, He promises to make His presence known.

READY, AIM, FIRE

I once heard a man sum up his whole life with these words: "Ready, aim...ready, aim...ready, aim..." He never got to *fire!* His entire Christian life was learning and getting ready, but he never actually did anything for the Lord. He never got out there and lived the Christian life he'd been learning about.

If God's purpose is to conform us to the image of His Son, we must go where He's going *now.* The second mile is where He walks *now.*

The greatest example of being conformed to the image of Christ is found in this statement from Paul:

> I have been crucified with Christ; it is no longer I who live, but *Christ lives in me;* and the life which I now live in the flesh I live by faith in the Son of God, who loved me and gave Himself for me. (Galatians 2:20)

That's God's ultimate goal for our lives—to allow Christ to live His life in our mortal bodies. And the time to do that is *now.*

THE VIEW FROM THE SECOND MILE: SEEING GOD'S PURPOSE

If you want to be like Christ, you must be where He is and do what He's doing. Just calling yourself a Christian is not enough.

Jesus once turned to those who were following Him and said, "Why do you keep calling Me 'Lord, Lord,' and not do the things which I say?" (Luke 6:46). The Christian life must be lived on God's terms, recognizing that He's trying to conform you to the image of Christ; that's His purpose. For the world doesn't need to see good people doing good things for their God; they need to see Christ in you. When He is lifted up in our mortal bodies, He'll draw all men to Himself.

When people see your life, what do they see? Or perhaps it's better stated, *who* do they see? Do not simply ask, "What would Jesus do?" but "What is Jesus doing through my life?"

CHAPTER FOUR

BREAKING THE ONE-MILE BARRIER

Seeing God's Invitation

Come to Me.

Matthew 11:28

When my daughter Sarah was four, she had a favorite saying: "I can do it!" It was true—she could do anything! You name it: Put her shoes on, get her pajamas on, brush her teeth, pour the milk. She could walk by herself to the playground, drive herself to the church, fly an airplane, or go to the moon. Translated, her words "I can do it!" meant, "Dad, I don't want any help."

I remember the day she was trying to open a bottle of pop. I moved toward her to offer some help, but she quickly blurted out, "Dad, I can do it!" The fact was that she couldn't do it. Her little hands didn't have the strength necessary to turn the cap. Finally she looked up into my eyes and asked, "Dad, can you help me?" She gave the problem over to me, her dad. And had I somehow chosen *not* to help her, she couldn't have sampled the refreshing taste of that drink.

As determined as Sarah is, she's smart enough to know when she needs help, and she's willing to ask for it. That's the exact point where she surpasses many adults in the world today. For we are *not* self-sufficient, no matter what we say. There are many people who either don't know they need help, or have too much pride to ask for help, who are missing out on having abundant life in Christ.

LETTING JESUS TAKE OVER

There's much more God intended for us to experience in life, but no person can do it by themselves…they need Christ.

> Life on the second mile doesn't get more hectic; it gets much more peaceful.

The second mile is not about more activity or harder work…it's about being in relationship with Christ. And as a result, life on the second mile doesn't get more hectic; it gets much more peaceful. The second mile is where you let go and Jesus takes over.

The only way to break the one-mile barrier is to give your life completely to Christ.

Let's look at another Scripture where I believe Jesus reveals what it looks like to walk with Him on the second mile. In this passage, Jesus gives us an amazing invitation:

> Come to Me, all you who labor and are heavy laden, and I will give you rest. Take My yoke upon you and learn from Me, for I am gentle and lowly in heart, and you will find rest for your souls. For My Yoke is easy and My burden is light. (Matthew 11:28–30)

But before Jesus gives us this information, He sets it up in context with these words of prayer to His Father:

> I thank You, Father, Lord of heaven and earth, that You have hidden these things from the wise and prudent and have revealed them to babes. Even so, Father, for so it seemed good in Your sight. All things have been delivered to Me by My Father, and no one knows the Son except the Father. Nor does anyone know the Father except the Son, and the one to whom the Son wills to reveal Him. (Matthew 11:25–27)

He is saying, "Father, You have chosen to hide the things of the kingdom from the wise and to reveal them to those the world considers childish. You resist the proud and give to the meek. You allow those who think they have it all figured out to live under that delusion, but You freely give to those who recognize their need and who ask of You."

Those who are wise in the world are crippled by their knowledge. They're used to understanding everything, and they assume they can also figure out the ways of God, as if God was just another deduction from well-reasoned arguments. But God, who is Spirit…God, who is the Creator of all people…God, who is beyond our simple minds…cannot be figured out, unless we humble ourselves and call out to God for help.

> When you walk with Christ on the second mile,
> He'll bring complete rest to your soul.

This is a theme that's carried throughout Jesus' teaching. Unless you become as a little child—believing there's something you don't know, and realizing that the knowledge you possess isn't final—you cannot enter the kingdom of God. But when you come to Christ, you discover that everything you need is found in Him. When you walk with Christ on the second mile, He'll bring your soul to complete rest.

But if we're to find that complete rest in the midst of serving Him, He requires that we do three things:

[handwritten: childlike means open. You realize you do not know everything.]

1. Come.

2. Take His yoke.

3. Learn from Him.

If we don't do all three, we will not find rest for our soul.

THE FIRST REQUIREMENT

[handwritten: Mindset . Come.]

The first requirement of walking with Jesus is to "come."

Jesus does not primarily say to us, "Do this" and "Don't do that." He tells us, *"Come to Me."*

We often would rather go and do something for Him than simply come to Him. For we aren't sure we want to be where He is. We aren't sure we want to hear what He might say. We would rather be doing something that's on our heart rather than being always interested in what's on His heart. But He's the Master, and we're the servants—when He says come, we must come.

That may seem too simple, but it's a huge barrier for many people. Jesus is saying, "I've come that you might have abundant life, so come and receive it. There's nothing too big for Me, and nothing too small for Me." But He doesn't dispense this abundant life like medicine; it is found *in Him.* You don't drop by and get a quick fix; rather, rest for your soul is found by abiding *in His presence.* As long as you remain in Him, He'll bring rest to your soul.

But to remain in Him, you have to start by simply coming to Jesus.

I've heard people say, "I don't understand this Christianity thing."

I ask, "Have you ever come to Jesus and given Him your life?"

"Well, no."

"Then you'll never understand rest for your soul."

The initial requirement is to step out in faith and come. You see, the two categories of people are not the intellectual and the simple; the two categories of humanity are the willing and the unwilling. We must be willing to come. That's the first step on the second mile.

I met with a medical doctor who was struggling to release control of his life and to come to Jesus. He's a man who's used to being in charge. He worked in emergency medicine and made his living by taking charge and making the tough decisions. He had a beautiful family, a nice home, and a strong career, and was unwilling to turn things over to anybody else—including God.

One day he told me, "I like to be in charge. It's just how I'm made."

"That isn't true," I challenged Him. "*God* made you, and He made you for a relationship with Himself. Anything that hinders this relationship is sin. But if your problem is sin, there's a solution: Jesus came to save you from your sin."

"I guess I don't have any excuse then, do I?" he responded.

"None that God cannot deal with," I answered.

That night he decided to put his life in God's hands. For the first time...he was *willing* to follow Jesus.

Are you willing to come to Jesus? That's where it all begins; that's the first step onto the second mile. It's nothing less than a step of faith...and "without faith it is impossible to please Him" (Hebrews 11:6).

WHAT IS FAITH?

I'm convinced that many people don't know what biblical faith is. Let me tell you what faith is *not*.

First, faith is not a one-time decision at the time of your salvation. Such a decision does indeed require faith, but that's not the finish line as far as faith is concerned.

Second, faith is not making your best plans, then trusting God to bless them. That's nothing more than using God as a good-luck charm. Faith isn't asking God to bless *your* plans. God isn't obligated to bless our goals and dreams. Rather, we are to adjust to *His* plan for our life. We must respond to *His* activity. He's the Master, and we're His servants.

Third, faith is not crying out to God when your life falls apart. Faith isn't simply a last-ditch hope when you find yourself in a circumstance out of your control. That isn't walking by faith; that's desperation. That's saying, "If all else fails, I'll trust God." Or, "As a last resort, maybe God will help." Or, "When there's nowhere else to turn, I'll try God." Do you know people like this? When things are fine, God is never in the picture. When their life falls apart, when they've failed in all their plans, only then do they turn to God for help. But that's not faith.

✦ This is faith: <u>Active obedience to God's will for your life.</u>

Biblical faith is choosing to respond to God's will for our lives in practical living. It's choosing to obey God when the circumstances seem impossible to overcome. It's choosing to trust God contrary to human reasoning. It's choosing to deny self, pick up your cross, and follow His will for your life.

✦ Faith isn't real until it moves from your head to your heart and you act upon what God has said. That means we must be willing to rearrange our lives, making the necessary adjustments in order to obey God's will. And only when we count the cost will we experience the mighty power of God.

ANSWER YES

I have a good friend from Arkansas who had to wrestle with the decision to step out in faith and follow the Lord onto the second mile. Life was good. Bo was a young man with a lovely wife, three children, a new home, a degree in business, and a secure job as the controller of the family business overseeing funeral homes and a life insurance company. He was a good man, faithful in church, and always ready to do what any Christian would do.

When he heard about a mission trip to Canada, he was intrigued. Something inside him began to stir, and Bo knew this trip was God's invitation to be a part of something significant. So he went to Canada with a team of people to work with a small mission church of which I was the pastor at the time.

Each morning before the team would start their work for the day, I would lead in a devotional. Each morning was a special time with the group, but one day in particular it was as if God was speaking directly to Bo. Later, he couldn't stop thinking about what he had heard that morning. Even after he returned home to Arkansas, the word he'd received followed him and wouldn't let him go.

He knew he had to answer BEFORE learning more about what God was calling him to.

The message the Lord had for him was to answer a simple question of lordship. And Bo knew he had to give his answer to this question *before* he would learn more details about what God was calling him to. If Christ truly was the Lord of his life, he had to say *yes* before he knew what the Lord was going to ask him.

❧ For the major assignments in life, the Lord requires a heart of ready obedience before He'll reveal His own heart to us. He doesn't waste time speaking of deep things concerning the kingdom of God to a person who isn't already committed to respond. In fact, it would be better to be kept in the dark than to know what God is asking and choose not to respond.

Bo gave his response: "Lord, whatever You ask me to do, the answer is yes."

At that moment, the Lord clearly spoke: "I'm asking you to walk away from your business and follow me into full-time Christian service."

Although this thought had never before crossed Bo's mind, there was no hesitation, for he'd already given his answer. He and his family packed up and headed for seminary.

That decision put him on a road leading to study at a seminary in Canada. Not only that, he now serves alongside me as an associate pastor. Together, along with others whom God has brought to the church, we've seen many amazing things by the hand of God. As together we walk the second mile, I often hear Bo say, "I would never have known God like this if I hadn't said yes before I knew what He would ask." If he hadn't made the decision to follow Jesus, he would still be helping people at death rather than helping them live an abundant life with the Lord.

No Hesitation

The first step on the second mile is to come to Jesus. But you cannot come with reservations or a divided heart. When the Lord speaks, He doesn't want you to hesitate but to obey. Jesus said, "Come"—that's where it all begins.

 If God works in our lives according to our faith—how much can He do in you?

Your life today is a reflection of your faith—active obedience to God's will. Jesus often said to those who came to Him for help, "According to your faith let it be to you" (Matthew 9:29; see also Matthew 8:13; 9:22; 15:28; Mark 10:52; Luke 7:50). If God works also in *your* life according to your faith—how much can He do?

Jesus said, "Did I not say to you that if you would believe you would see the glory of God?" (John 11:40). Do you simply live a good life and come to church to give praise to God? God wants you to do more than give praise; He wants you to listen to Him, believe Him, respond to Him, and see His glory in your life as you live according to His will.

No Doubt

So why is it so many people don't walk the second mile and fail to see the mighty power of God?

There may be many reasons, but a big one is doubt. Whereas *faith* reveals the glory of God, *doubt* removes you from God's activity. When you look at the Bible, you see men and women following God and receiving the blessing of being His people. But as soon as they questioned Him, as soon as they trusted in their own ability over God's ability, as soon as they doubted His word, *they lost it all.*

God's word for you is not a suggestion or an option among many ideas…it is your life!

Doubting God is foolishness! Doubting removes us from God's activity, for He'll respond only to people of faith. The Bible tells us to "ask in faith, with no doubting, for he who doubts is like a wave of the sea driven and tossed by the wind. For let not that man suppose that he will receive anything from the Lord; he is a double-minded man, unstable in all his ways" (James 1:6–8).

Circumstances in life can seem insurmountable…*if* your eyes are on circumstances. The criticism of men will be discouraging…*if* you're listening to them. But if instead your eyes are firmly fixed on Christ, and your ears are listening to His voice…you'll know peace.

No Fear

Closely aligned with doubt is fear. People really do want to live with significance and purpose; they really do want to please the Lord. But too often they're afraid to let go of their control. They're afraid of what the Lord might ask them to do, afraid they'll only fail if they attempt something beyond their ability, and afraid to step out of a comfortable life and rely on the Lord for their needs.

But the closer a person walks with Christ, the more their fear dissipates. "There is no fear in love; but perfect love casts out fear" (1 John 4:18).

The Christian life is far more than being a good person: It's a lifestyle of walking with Christ day by day. That's the only life that will please God. It's the only life that will make you right with God.

The only way to break the one-mile barrier is to trust Jesus with your life.

You cannot walk the second mile in your own strength. The only way to break the one-mile barrier is to take a step of faith and trust Jesus with your life. No amount of enthusiasm will ever stand up to the rigors of the second mile. Only one thing will bear the strain, and that's a personal relationship with Jesus Christ.

Consider these words that A. W. Tozer prayed on the day of his ordination:

> O God, quicken to life every power within me, that I may lay hold on eternal things. Open my eyes that I may see; give me acute spiritual perception; enable me to taste Thee and know that Thou art good. Make heaven more real to me than any earthly thing has ever been.
>
> O God and Father, I repent of my sinful preoccupation with visible things. The world has been too much with me. Thou hast been here and I knew it not. I have been blind to Thy presence. Open my eyes that I may behold Thee in and around me. For Christ's sake, Amen.

THE VIEW FROM THE SECOND MILE: SEEING GOD'S INVITATION

God, by His grace, offers abundant life in Christ. It is received through faith when you choose to come to Him.

As you come, you stand on the threshold of a completely new life that can be found only with Christ. In the midst of all the distractions and the many people from the world who would give you counsel, you must look into the eyes of Jesus.

Do you trust Him? Do you believe He loves you? Are you convinced He'll give you abundant life?

If so, then you must choose. His hand is outstretched toward your life and you must respond.

The decision to step onto the second mile is only one prayer away.

Today, I want you to hear Jesus say, "Come." Before He ever tells you where He wants to take you, you must give Him your answer.

"Yes, Lord…I come"—will that be your answer?

CHAPTER FIVE

IN STEP WITH CHRIST

Seeing God's Strength

Take My yoke upon you and learn from Me,

for I am gentle and lowly in heart.

Matthew 11:29

Jesus came from the right hand of the Father to meet us where we were. If we want to find God in all His fullness, we must travel the same road Jesus walked when He came down to us. It's a narrow road, one that few choose to walk, as Jesus indicated: "Enter by the narrow gate; for wide is the gate and broad is the way that leads to destruction, and there are many who go in by it. Because narrow is the gate and difficult is the way which leads to life, and there are few who find it" (Matthew 7:13–14).

But take courage. You don't walk alone. Jesus is still on the road, and He'll lead you to enjoy a blessed relationship with His heavenly Father.

 To follow Christ always means forward progress.

The essence of being a Christian is to follow Christ. The word *follow* indicates movement, a change, or perhaps a new direction in life. A stagnant life is the result of staying where you are, but to follow Christ always means forward progress—and with Christ always in sight.

While the first step is simply to come to Him, there are many more steps to take along the journey.

You'll quickly discover that the Christian life is lived on God's terms. When we follow Christ, we can't pick and choose what we want to do and what we don't want to do. He is absolute Lord of our lives.

IT ISN'T EASY

When it comes to the decision to follow Jesus, He doesn't make it easy. Sometimes I fear we're giving a false impression of what it means to be a Christian. The decision for salvation that people make can be based on a wrong motive because we tell only half the story and leave them with an impression of our faith that isn't true.

For example, we may say to a person who's contemplating their mortality, "Would you rather go to heaven or hell? If you want to go to heaven, come follow Jesus. He knows the way."

Or perhaps we say to a person who's overwhelmed with life, "Do you want to struggle with anxiety, stress, and burnout, or do you want peace in your heart? Come follow Jesus. He's the Prince of Peace."

Or to a person who's facing a great challenge, "The Bible says, 'If God is for us, who can be against us?' (Romans 8:31). Do you want God to be on your side? If you want the power of God in your life, come follow Jesus, because through Him we become children of God."

Or to an older adult, "How's your retirement? Would you like to inherit the kingdom of heaven? If you want to live in a mansion forever, come follow Jesus. The riches of the kingdom are for His people."

You can easily see why some people are left with the impression that being a Christian is simply accepting all the good things God wants to give us, with no thought of what we give to Him.

Now everything I said above is true: Jesus *is* the way to heaven and the Prince of Peace; He *does* bring us into the family of God, and we inherit the kingdom of heaven. But that isn't the point! Christianity is not just about the good things we receive…but about a relationship with God through Jesus Christ whereby He is Lord.

Oh, I know that, you may be thinking. *Jesus is Lord.* No,

I'm not talking about the theological statement "Jesus is Lord," but about a description of your life: Is Jesus *your* Lord, *your* Master, *your* life, so that you live to please Him and to obey Him, and to respond to everything He says because of your love for Him?

What worries me is that some people marvel over the great testimonies of how *other people* have followed God, yet it never crosses their own mind that God would call them to follow with equal commitment. When Jesus says *follow,* He means *follow!*

Following Jesus as your Lord may mean sacrifice, giving up things you enjoy, leaving behind that which you love for someone you love more. It means going the second mile.

When Jesus said, "Come to Me...and I will give you rest," we misunderstand what He's saying. He isn't saying God will give you a life of ease and take away all your hardships. He isn't implying that He'll never ask you to do anything difficult or anything that pushes you beyond your abilities and talents. Instead, Jesus promises to sustain you and cause you to stand firm no matter what the circumstance. He'll strengthen your life and give you the energy to keep going.

TAKE HIS YOKE

The first word we've considered in going the second mile is *come.* The second word is *take.*

You've entered a relationship with Christ whereby you and
He walk together, side by side.

Once we come to Jesus, the next thing we do is to "take
His yoke" upon you. That's when life gets really exciting; that's
when you start to see the activity of God in your life. For it
means you've entered a relationship with Christ whereby you
and He walk together, side by side.

Many people have come to Jesus, but few are willing to
actually take His yoke upon them.

I sometimes hear people whimpering with a pitiful tone
and saying, "I'm suffering for Jesus, and I don't know how
much more I can take." Where's the majesty and power of
Christ in that? The Bible says, "In Him dwells all the fullness
of the Godhead bodily; and you are complete in Him, who is
the head of all principality and power" (Colossians 2:9–10).
To be yoked with Christ is to have all the resources of heaven
at your side.

I realize some people today may not know the term *yoke*
as it was used in the Bible. I'm not referring to *yolk*—the yel-
low of an egg. To "take Jesus' yoke" doesn't mean you become
an egghead—a little bit scrambled—or that you now live life
sunny-side up. No, *yoke* is an agricultural term. It was used to
link a team of oxen as they would pull a plow or a cart or some
type of heavy load.

A yoke couples two oxen together, but it doesn't exempt
either from work; rather, it makes the work manageable.

In our lives, there's work to be done and there are burdens we all must endure. Indeed, the second mile can be hard work, very tiring, and emotionally draining. But the Christian doesn't do it alone; he or she is yoked to Christ. As we walk with Him, He takes the load and accomplishes the task with us.

So how do you take the yoke? Perhaps the chief struggle at this point is not rebellion, but lack of understanding. We just don't know how to do it or what it means.

To communicate with people, Jesus often used illustrations about common, everyday things. In the first century, everyone understood taking a yoke. A yoke was essentially a solid wooden bar stretched across two oxen and fastened around their necks. It was common in Jesus' day to see an ox working with a young calf running by her side. The mature ox would be available to satisfy the thirst of the calf, and the calf would become stronger and stronger as it grew. The calf was free from any rope or yoke; it just enjoyed the simple life.

 His life was no longer his own. He belonged to another and must yield to another's desires.

But there would be a day when fun and games were over and the young ox was ready to work. In reality, the only purpose of raising an ox is for the work to be done. When the day arrives to become a part of the farmer's work, the ox is introduced to the yoke. A mature and experienced ox would stand quietly in the yoke, while the young ox would come alongside her. But the thought of losing its freedom to run in any direction, of having to exchange that freedom for a yoke, isn't easy to accept. So the young ox would be "encouraged" through many means to bend its neck and yield. Once the ox slipped into the yoke and was locked in, his life was no longer his own. He now belonged to another and must yield to another's desires.

That's the image that came into mind for those who heard Jesus speak. This is the truth that many do not understand. We hear Jesus say, "Come to Me," and we willingly come to find freedom from sin. We find joy in His presence and gorge ourselves on the spiritual food He provides. Then He says, "Take my yoke," and we hesitate. We rather enjoy running around as we please, just like a young calf full of life.

Nevertheless, if we're to walk the second mile, we must come to Jesus and take His yoke upon us. It's a great thing to come to Jesus and be born again. But there comes a point when we move out of our infantile state and engage in the work of the kingdom.

Many have "come" but not "taken." Many have been born, but not yet yoked. But either we serve self or we serve the Lord. Jesus said, "If anyone desires to come after Me, let him deny himself, take up his cross, and follow Me" (Matthew 16:24). If you refuse to take His yoke, and yield your freedom to His will for your life, you cannot walk the second mile with Christ.

We must take His yoke, but it's a choice He gives us to make.

We weren't born so we could run around as we please; the reason for our existence is to do the will of the heavenly Father.

YOKED TOGETHER

The joy of the yoke, however, is found in walking with Jesus. In a yoke of oxen, there's always a leader who's seasoned by years of experience. Notice that Jesus said, "Take *My* yoke upon you." It's *His* yoke; *He* is the leader. When you realize the He's still under the yoke doing the work of His Father, you discover wonderful courage. He's still on the job, and we have the privilege of laboring alongside Him as "God's fellow workers" (1 Corinthians 3:9).

 If we don't adjust to what Christ is doing in our world, we'll never see what God planned for our life.

Christ invites us to work *with* Him as He fulfills the eternal purposes of His Father. Our problem is that we run around doing work *for* Christ just as we please. Like an immature calf, we wander through life following our own plans, and it never crosses our minds to let Christ direct our lives. But if we keep choosing not to adjust to what Christ is doing in our world, we'll never see what God had planned for our life, we'll never experience what God could have done through our life, and we'll find ourselves all alone. The result: No rest.

If you want God to take you beyond yourself and into the place of the divine, you cannot refuse the yoke. And although there are restrictions from which our flesh will always try and break free, if we're faithful to learn from Him, His promise will be fulfilled: We *will* find rest for our souls.

I remember walking down the road with my son Stephen when he was little. We would walk side by side, hand in hand. As he would reach way up, I would hold on tight to keep him from stumbling as he learned to walk. He was notorious for falling headlong, adding to a long history of bumps and bruises. He would inevitably catch his foot on a crack, stumble, and fall. But as long as we were holding hands, I would catch him before any damage was done.

After one of these rescues, I remember how he looked up and said, "I'm sure glad I was holding your hand, Dad." We were holding hands, all right. But his safety wasn't in the fact that *he held my hand*, but that *I held his*. He didn't have the strength to hold on to me, but I had the strength to hold on to him. We were partners, but I carried the load.

When Stephen was a bit older, I remember one day in particular when we were walking together on a mountain trail. Stephen had wanted to run along ahead of me. But eventually we came to a part of the trail that dropped steeply before us. It was rocky, slippery, and a little scary. I asked, "Stephen, should we go down there?" He hesitated, then said, "Can I hold your hand?"

As we walk with Jesus, our confidence is not that we're holding His hand, but that He's holding ours. We don't have the strength; *He* does. It's not that we are yoked to Him but that He is yoked to us. For when we take His yoke, we know His power.

CHOOSING HIS CONTROL

The key is that you must take His yoke; *you* must put it on, not begrudgingly but willingly. This word *take* literally means "to lift up from the ground in order to carry." It's a readiness and willingness to accept a task.

In the same way, Jesus said that whoever refuses to take up their cross and come after Him cannot be His disciple (Luke 14:27). Your cross is not a burden you bear. It's the decision to pick up the Father's will for your life. The cross was the Father's will for Jesus; He had a choice to make, and He chose obedience. Likewise, we must choose the yoke and get in step with Jesus.

 God will never force His will upon your life.

You'll find that God will never force His will upon your life. But if you don't take it, if you choose not to walk with Him, you'll miss out on so much.

The image of taking the yoke of Christ means being completely under His control. Can you see the picture of the yoke? Once you choose Christ you cannot turn back, nor can you stay where you are. Wherever Jesus goes, you're right there with Him.

ONE WITH CHRIST

The further implication of the yoke is that you cannot live a sinful lifestyle and walk with Him at the same time. You must leave the world behind. The image of the yoke is that of being *at one with Christ.*

All I do should be based on a perfect oneness with Him, not on a self-willed determination to be godly. If what you do for the Lord is burdensome, you're doing it alone; you're not yoked with Him. Being one with Christ will bring joy in the midst of trial.

Listen to the Lord's promise:

Abide in Me, and I in you. As the branch cannot bear fruit of itself, unless it abides in the vine, neither can you, unless you abide in Me. I am the vine, you are the branches. He who abides in Me, and I in him,

bears much fruit; for without Me you can do nothing…. These things I have spoken to you, that My
joy may remain in you, and that your joy may be full.
(John 15:4–5, 11)

When we abide in Christ all things are possible, and our
joy will be full. I'm convinced that those who have chosen to
take the yoke of Christ cannot complain. They're shoulder to
shoulder with Christ, and when they're walking with Him in
this way, all authority in heaven and on earth is present in their
lives.

When we choose to come and take up the Father's will, we
learn from Jesus what life's all about. The only way to handle
life is to learn from Him: "Take My yoke upon you and *learn
from Me,*" Jesus says (Matthew 11:29).

Jesus carried a great burden, but He shared it with the
Father. When we learn from Him, we know the strength of
God in our lives. No power can conquer the Spirit of God living within the human spirit; it creates an inner invincibility to
be used for His glory. But you cannot learn from Him unless
you first take His yoke upon you.

CHRIST UNDERSTANDS THIS ROAD

We cannot walk the second mile alone; we must remain with
Christ. He understands that road, for He walked it Himself.

Christ did not have to leave the throne room of God and come to a fallen earth, but He chose to come anyway. And after arriving on earth in a physical body, He continued to walk on the second mile. He could have been born in a palace, but He chose the stable in Bethlehem. He could have been raised among royalty, but He chose a carpenter's family. He could have enjoyed great wealth, but He chose poverty. He could have gained great fame, but He chose an unpopular message. He could have called down a legion of angels for His protection, but He chose to be taken into the hands of sinful men.

> In choosing the second mile as His way of life,
> He also chose death on a cross.

He's the author of all life—"All things were created through Him and for Him. And He is before all things, and in Him all things consist" (Colossians 1:16–17). But in choosing the second mile as His own way of life, He also chose death on a cross.

WITHOUT COMPLAINING

You can always tell those who are walking in the strength of the Lord because they *don't complain* over life's burdens. They've learned from Jesus, and they have inner peace and joy that comes from their relationship with Christ.

It's good to look back and see the difference Christ makes in your daily life. My wife and I had a stretch of time where it seemed as though everything was going wrong. It started out with a flood in our community that was the worst ever recorded in our area. The basement of our home was severely damaged by water, but this "act of God" wasn't covered by our home insurance. Unfortunately, all of our children had their bedrooms in the basement, and they were all displaced.

During the three months it took to renovate the home, we experienced a series of other mishaps: The hot water tank rusted through and began to leak, our daughter had an accident on a friend's four-wheeler and hurt her arm, the stock waterer for the horses froze up and stopped working, one of our horses went lame, and my wife's back went out and she could hardly move for two months.

Then, while visiting another church when we were on vacation, our minivan was hit in the parking lot by a teenage girl with no insurance. Returning home from vacation, we discovered that the electrical breaker to the freezer in the garage tripped off and a quarter side of beef had thawed and rotted. At the same time, we had a large and unexpected bill from the tax man. And to top it all off, the family dog of thirteen years died.

 Feeling sorry for ourselves never crossed our mind.

As we scrambled to deal with all that was happening in our lives, my wife and I had a strange awakening. There wasn't an ounce of our being that wanted to complain. While others felt sorry for us, feeling sorry for ourselves never crossed our mind. It was as if the Lord wanted each of us to fully know this truth: "The nearness of God is my good" (Psalm 73:28, NASB). Nothing else mattered. It was one of the most freeing experiences to see this evidence that Christ was with us, and everything was going to be okay. He truly brings rest for the soul, when unrest prevails all around us.

THE VIEW FROM THE SECOND MILE: SEEING GOD'S STRENGTH

Can you hear the Lord's invitation? Jesus is saying to you, "Is your soul tired, restless, uneasy? Then come to Me…take My yoke upon you and learn from Me."

What makes a soul weary? What is it that causes a soul to be restless? Simply this: You've come and found new life, but have not yet yoked with Christ. You may be born again, but you've wandered off from His presence and followed your own dreams.

Beware of allowing the influence of your friends or your circumstances to separate you from the Lord. It will sap your strength and slow your spiritual growth. When you seek to produce what only Christ can do, the price you pay is frustration, disappointment, decreasing effort, and a lowering of standards.

Do you recognize that you feel bitter and frustrated and are easily offended? The fruit of the Spirit is slipping away, for you've fallen away from the closeness of Christ.

The yoke of Jesus isn't burdensome; it makes you one with Him. He'll bring abundant life.

Are you spiritually tired? Is there a restlessness in your soul? Does the thought of a second mile cause you to tremble? Don't fear; the second mile means hearing Jesus say, "Come to Me, walk with Me, and learn from Me the meaning of life—and I will give rest to your soul."

CHAPTER SIX

IN YOUR COUNTENANCE

Seeing God's Joy

These things I have spoken to you, that My joy
may remain in you, and that your joy may be full.

John 15:11

When I was a teenager trying to figure out my faith, the Lord brought a man into my life who made a huge impact. Jack was an airplane mechanic by trade and built race cars and powerboats as a hobby. He had a brilliant mind and could fix anything.

Meanwhile I had a car that was in constant need of repair, and I often found myself in trouble, looking for help. One particular evening I called Jack for some advice on fixing my engine, and he decided to come over and give me a hand.

It was a cold night and there was no heat in my garage. The job was a difficult one that was causing much frustration. At one point, Jack had his body contorted into an uncomfortable position, trying to loosen a bolt that wasn't going to budge. He gave one last torque with all his might and the wrench slipped off, driving his knuckles into the engine block. When he pulled his hand out, the skin had been peeled back and blood was starting to flow. What came out of his mouth left me absolutely stunned!

By the way, before I go on, I need to mention that Jack was not just a mechanic, but a deacon in our church. Here I was, an impressionable young teenager trying to find my way spiritually, and I saw firsthand what kind of faith that deacon really had. There's nothing like driving your knuckles onto a frozen engine block to discover what it means to be born again!

Before this deacon could think about what he said, guess what had slipped out of his mouth? He said, "Praise God!"

I thought to myself, *You've got to be kidding me! What a weirdo! That isn't right!* I was feeling the pain, and it wasn't even my knuckles!

I saw something that night that left an impression on me: Jack was different. I saw that there was something inside him controlling his heart, and no circumstance could shake him. His faith was real, and it made a difference in the real world of a mechanic.

Jack never really talked to me about spiritual things, but I'll never forget the joy in his life…and I wanted it.

A Concern for Joy

I want you to grasp something very important about the second mile. When Christ forgives your sin and fills you with His spirit, you ought to know the *joy of the Lord* in your life. Did you know the Lord is very concerned about your joy as you walk the second mile?

The word *gospel* means "good news." Those who know the good news of God and have entered into a personal relationship with Jesus Christ will be filled with the joy of the Lord. He wants all Christians to be full of joy. He wants their lives to display, before a watching world, the difference Christ can make.

Consider the high priestly prayer of Jesus in John 17, where He poured out His heart to the heavenly Father. This prayer came in the last hours before Jesus would endure betrayal, illegal trials, beatings, and crucifixion. He realized His hour had come, and He would face His most difficult assignment from the Father. He had done faithfully all that had been asked of Him, but His assignment in the flesh was coming to a close.

As He talked with the Father, Jesus turned His prayer toward the disciples. The first thing He prayed for them was this: "that they may have My joy fulfilled in themselves" (John 17:13).

Think of the importance of this moment: As these disciples go, so goes the winning of a world. All that Christ accomplished on the cross to redeem the world would be given into the hands of these men to proclaim. They were the church!

 Their faces would testify that there's freedom from sin and hope in Christ.

Knowing what had been entrusted to the disciples, His prayer is amazing. Notice that Jesus didn't pray, "Father, make them to be great preachers, for they will proclaim the gospel." He didn't pray, "Father, give them insight to teach theology to those who will come." No, what was on the heart of Jesus was to pray, "Father, place *My joy* in them, that *their joy* may be made full." Why was the Lord concerned about their being full of joy? Because He knew their countenance would validate the message of abundant life in Christ. Their faces would testify that there's freedom from sin and hope in Christ.

Jesus knew there would be many difficult days ahead for the disciples, and the watching world would see how they responded. The disciples would prove that a relationship with God brings joy and that everything else pales in comparison to a relationship with Christ. By their joy they would proclaim, "Cast your insults and revile me, but God is near. Throw me in prison, but God is near. Stone me and beat me, but the nearness of God is my good." Their joy would affirm how they could never exchange their salvation for anything on earth!

Because of the *look in the eyes* of those who proclaimed the gospel, people would hear it and believe it.

His Joy Is Ours

Yes, Jesus was concerned about joy in the disciples' lives…and He's concerned about joy in *your* life! Are you?

Look at a few other passages of Scripture to see how important joy is for Christians as they walk the second mile.

> I am the vine, you are the branches. He who abides in Me, and I in him, bears much fruit; for without Me you can do nothing…. These things I have spoken to you, that My *joy* may remain in you, and that your *joy* may be full. (John 15:5, 11)

> Until now you have asked nothing in My name. Ask, and you will receive, that your *joy* may be full. (John 16:24)

> May the God of hope fill you with all *joy* and peace in believing, that you may abound in hope by the power of the Holy Spirit. (Romans 15:13)

But the fruit of the Spirit is love, *joy*, peace, longsuffering, kindness, goodness, faithfulness, gentleness, self-control. (Galatians 5:22–23)

These things we write to you that your *joy* may be full. (1 John 1:4)

Rejoice in the Lord always. Again I will say, *rejoice!*" (Philippians 4:4)

Count it all *joy* when you fall into various trials. (James 1:2)

So they departed from the presence of the council, *rejoicing* that they were counted worthy to suffer shame for His name. (Acts 5:41)

 If you've lost the joy of the Lord, you're in trouble!

Let me suggest that if you've lost the joy of the Lord, you've lost the presence of the Holy Spirit in your life. I'm not talking about losing your salvation, but losing the joy of your salvation. If you've lost the joy of serving the Lord, you're in trouble! For the Lord has given you the Holy Spirit to help you have joy.

JOY COMES FROM TRUST

Do you know why I can have joy? Why I tend to be optimistic and positive in life? Because I trust the Lord. I know He's sovereign and on His throne. The Father gave to Jesus all authority in heaven and on earth, and that means I'm in good hands. He's in absolute control of all things. Furthermore, I know He sees what I don't see. He has the big picture and knows what's coming. And I know He loves me.

To trust the Lord and to be filled with joy, however, can be hard when you're in a situation that's overwhelming.

Imagine telling the disciples to have joy when they were caught in a terrible storm while sailing on the Sea of Galilee. They got into the boat and launched out because Jesus told them to. Now their lives were in danger. Among these men were seasoned fishermen who knew the sea well, and their conclusion was this: "We are perishing!" (Matthew 8:25). I can imagine their thinking: *The only reason we're out in this storm is because we obeyed the Lord. Why did we listen to Jesus? He's only a carpenter, but we're fishermen. We knew better. He's put our lives in danger and there's no way out!*

Where's the joy?

Or tell Mary and Martha to have joy after Lazarus, their brother, had died. Jesus could have come and healed Lazarus, but He didn't come when they really needed Him. In fact, Scripture indicates that He chose *not* to come until after

Lazarus died (John 11:6). Can you imagine what might have gone through Mary and Martha's minds? *I thought Jesus loved Lazarus. I thought He cared about our family. After all we've done for Him, and He didn't find it in His heart to come in our time of need! Don't say Jesus loves us—He could have helped...but He didn't.*

Where's the joy?

Or tell the disciples to have joy after Jesus was crucified. They'd left everything to follow this Man, and now He was dead! Imagine what went through each of their minds: *I thought Jesus came to save the world, but He couldn't even save Himself! Now the authorities are looking for us! We believed in Him, but now He's gone. What do we do now?* Their world was turned upside down, and they were left hiding in fear.

Where's the joy?

In those three examples, was this desperation the end of the story?

Not at all.

Although the disciples were convinced they were going to die in the storm, Jesus stood and shouted, "Be still!" Nature yielded to His command, and all was calm.

Although Mary and Martha were convinced they would never see their brother again, Jesus came and said, "Lazarus, come forth!" And he came out of the grave alive.

Although the disciples were convinced their Lord was dead and all hope was gone, Jesus was resurrected. He came to them in the upper room and said, "Peace be with you." He was alive!

When life seemed out of control, everything
happened just as Jesus planned.

In all three situations, their sorrow, frustration, and disappointment were turned to awe, wonder, and joy like they'd never known before! Because in all three situations, everything happened just as Jesus had planned. He *was* in control when life seemed out of control.

The apostle Paul proclaimed, "We know that God causes all things to work together for good to those who love God, to those who are called according to His purpose" (Romans 8:28, NASB). That verse doesn't say, "All things work out just like we want them to." But it reminds us how God truly is in control. He is fulfilling His purposes in our lives.

I can have joy because I trust that God's will for my life is best. The gift of the Holy Spirit in my life means God is near, and the nearness of God is my good.

I know there are burdens to carry and times of heartache to endure. But when I'm weary and heavy laden, I don't forget the invitation of Jesus to come to Him in that situation, and He will give me rest. If I take His yoke upon me as He asks me to, and learn from the One who is gentle and humble in heart, I *will* find rest for my soul.

The Lord doesn't ask us to do things that are naturally easy for us; He will ask us to do only that which we're enabled to do through His grace. And His grace will sustain us.

LIGHTEN UP

I may be a little off here, but I think there are times when the Lord would say to us, "Lighten up! Don't be so uptight all the time! Why so downcast? Why so sad? Why do you act as if serving Me is so terrible? You have the privilege of sharing the good news!"

Think about it: How can we share good news with a bad attitude? For a downcast spirit nullifies the very message we proclaim.

The world needs to see good news in action. They need to see abundant life in Christ.

It was the joy of the Lord within the apostles that validated the message of the gospel. They were so full of the joy of salvation that we hear them say things like this: "To live is Christ and to die is gain" (Philippians 1:21). Or we see them singing even in the depths of a horrific prison (Acts 16:25). They could walk the second mile with joy—because joy doesn't come from circumstances, but from a relationship. They walked with Jesus, and He filled them full of His joy.

 Does your life demonstrate the GOOD news of God?

To all believers, God tells us through Scripture to "conduct yourselves in a manner worthy of the gospel of Christ" (Philippians 1:27, NASB). Are you living worthy of the gospel?

Does your life demonstrate the *good* news of God?

If you're walking on the second mile with Jesus, you'll have His joy. Joy is available to all who receive the Lord into their lives, and the difference should be obvious to all who encounter your life.

This joy comes not from a job well done, but from a relationship with Christ. You'll find it's much better to walk with the Lord than to perform great acts of self-sacrifice ("To obey is better than sacrifice" (1 Samuel 15:22).

When your heart is wholly committed to Him, He promises to make His presence known in your life: "The eyes of the LORD run to and fro throughout the whole earth, to *show Himself strong* on behalf of those who heart is loyal to Him" (2 Chronicles 16:9). It's His strong presence that brings joy.

FROM DARKNESS TO LIGHT

Let me tell you about a life-changing moment in my journey with Christ. I was twenty years old, working at a logging camp in northern Canada. We were involved in some dangerous work with chain saws in a remote part of a mountain range. It was January, very cold—thirty-five degrees below zero—and I was feeling pretty worn out after a long day's work.

Still a rookie on the job, I misjudged the pressure on a log as I cut into it. When it broke, it hit my leg with a force that sent me flying into a snowbank. The femur in my left leg was absolutely shattered.

The guys working with me put me into the back of a pickup truck, and we bounced down the mountain to seek help, which was many miles away. I discovered a level of pain I'd never known before. But as I lay in the back of that truck, I wanted to sing! I was filled with joy.

I know this makes no sense at all, and some might call it shock. I call it the Holy Spirit's presence in my life. My life turned from darkness to light.

You see, I'd been running from God at the time, and my life had been crumbling under the weight of sin. But in that moment of crisis I saw my life from God's perspective, and I repented of my sin immediately. The joy of forgiveness and a right relationship with God flooded my life with joy.

Paul taught the Colossian church to be "joyously giving thanks to the Father, who has qualified us to share in the inheritance of the saints in Light. For He rescued us from the domain of darkness, and transferred us to the kingdom of His beloved Son, in whom we have redemption, the forgiveness of sins" (Colossians 1:11–14, NASB).

That's the joy I experienced—knowing that I was taken out of darkness and into the presence of my Lord. I was redeemed, forgiven of my sin, and filled with unspeakable joy. It wasn't coming from my circumstance; it was coming from my relationship with Christ.

When a person has an encounter with the living Lord,

there ought to be a visible change in his life.

There's no greater barrier to the gospel than a bitter old sourpuss who claims to be a Christian. When Christ makes His home in your heart, He turns the lights on! Let His light shine. Let others see the difference Christ has made in your life.

A person who's on the second mile with Christ doesn't complain.

(I can easily tell a person who's on the second mile with Christ: They don't whine over every little thing. They're not easily offended, nor are they critical of others around them. They're content, and they're positive, for they have the joy of the Lord in their life.)

THE VIEW FROM THE SECOND MILE: SEEING GOD'S JOY

Earlier in this chapter I told the story of Jack, the mechanic. That incident in my garage happened over twenty years ago... and I still remember it. Jack's spirit that night left a living impression on me, a living demonstration that his faith was real.

That kind of joy cannot be found; it's given only by Jesus Christ. Joy is more than an emotion or feeling. It's the ability to see beyond any particular event to the sovereign Lord who stands above all events and ultimately has control over them. It means having a confidence that's rooted in faith. You can know this joy on the second mile when you have a keen awareness that the living Lord is present.

What impressions do you leave on other people? When they observe your life, do they sense that the gospel is "good news"? Are you a living example that the nearness of God is your good? What do they see when they look into your eyes?

Let me challenge you to spend enough time in the Lord's presence until you can truly "rejoice in the Lord always" (Philippians 4:4).

If you aren't concerned about being a joyful person, you need to be. If you don't know the condition of your countenance, find out. Try doing the following two things.

First, ask the Lord to show you. He'll search your heart and let you know what He finds. He's far more interested in your joy than you are.

Second, watch to see if people smile when they're around you. If you had a choice to be around someone who was negative versus someone who lifted you up, you would choose the person full of joy every time. People like to be around those who are positive and encouraging. Choose to be such a person. Ask the Lord to help your countenance reflect your relationship. For His presence in your life will bring light to a world of darkness.

CHAPTER SEVEN

IMPACTING THE REAL WORLD

Seeing God's Heart for Prayer

We do not wrestle against flesh and blood.
Ephesians 6:12

The Bible tells an amazing story, one that's beyond human comprehension without the Holy Spirit's illumination. It tells us how God came from heaven to earth to dwell among men. The Creator of all things came to His creation in the person of Jesus.

Jesus willingly laid aside all that was rightfully His, and He humbled Himself. He lived His life on this earth with all the limitations of the human condition, setting an example for us that we might know what God expects of our lives.

Let me put it another way: Jesus knows all things, and we ought to listen to Him! He came from eternity into time, revealing a perspective on reality that's absolutely true: We live in a spiritual world, and our time on earth is a temporary state that will give way to eternity. The life Jesus lived reflected the reality that nothing on earth is of value except that which is eternal.

PRAYER AND ETERNITY

The one who walks the second mile with Jesus will also reflect an eternal perspective that's keenly aware of the spiritual battle being waged for the souls of men and women: "We do not wrestle against flesh and blood, but against principalities, against powers, against the rulers of the darkness of this age, against spiritual hosts of wickedness in the heavenly places" (Ephesians 6:12). That is reality!

 The most significant activity in your life is to live in the reality of eternity.

Without any question, the most significant activity in your life is to live in the reality of eternity. Eternity is not a destination to go to after our physical bodies die; it's a sphere of reality in which we walk day by day. The person who doesn't pray is not living in the real world. That's why the second mile will lead you to the place of prayer. The greatest power in your life to influence the world is to go with Jesus to this most holy place.

It's a place Jesus knew well. Prayer isn't about mouthing words (although words are important in prayer); it isn't about religious discipline (although prayer takes discipline); and it isn't about promised benefits (though there are benefits). Prayer is about giving your life away to God and receiving life from God.

Jesus demonstrated throughout His life that prayer is first and foremost a relationship. He didn't go a day without prayer. I'm not talking about a quick "How ya doing, God?" as He ran out the door with toast and coffee. He spent great amounts of time in prayer with His heavenly Father. Everything in His life came from His time of prayer. Everything He did throughout the day had a direct link to what happened in prayer.

I know this is true, because the disciples noticed it. They realized there was something special about His prayer life that was different from anything they'd ever known.

The Bible records the moment when the disciples noticed the unique prayer life of Jesus. They saw a connection between the power in their Master's public life and the passion in His prayer life: "Now it came to pass, as He was praying in a certain place, when He ceased, that one of His disciples said to Him, "Lord, teach us to pray, as John also taught his disciples" (Luke 11:1).

The question they asked might cause one to think the disciples didn't know how to pray, but that's not the case. They'd grown up as devout Jews who had learned to pray as early as they could talk. They prayed regularly as a part of their life-style. What they were saying is this: "Jesus, we've been taught to pray since childhood; we've heard prayers from our parents, from our teachers, from our religious leaders. But there's something different about Your prayers. Lord, teach us to pray as You pray."

PRAYING AS JESUS PRAYED

The most important lesson to be learned on the second mile comes when you ask Jesus to teach you to pray as He did.

Did you know Jesus never taught His disciples to preach, only how to pray? Knowing how to speak to God is more important than knowing how to speak to men. If everything in your life is dependent upon Him, you must make knowing Him your first priority. Nothing else really matters.

The first lesson Jesus gave to the disciples was to pray, "Our Father." Prayer is first and foremost a relationship with God as our Father. We need to know we serve a God who loves us, cares for us, desires the best for us, and places value upon us. We come to Him in prayer as a child comes to his dad.

 In an intimate relationship with the heavenly Father, something happens when we pray: Heaven is moved.

When we're walking in an intimate relationship with the heavenly Father, seeking to obey His will for our lives, something happens when we pray: Heaven is moved. As we walk with Him, our lives are shaped into that which becomes a powerful channel of blessing. And we'll know whether we're walking with Him by what happens when we pray.

Listen to God's promise: "The effective, fervent prayer of a righteous man avails much" (James 5:16). Incredible! But note that this promise is for "a righteous man." When a *righteous* man prays, it's powerful. When an *un*righteous man prays, it's weak.

Put another way, when we allow sin into our lives and disobey God, when we hold on to unforgiveness in our heart, when we harbor bitterness against another person, when we've broken relationships with a brother or sister in Christ, when we gossip and allow jealousy into our lives…our prayers are nullified.

The apostle John wrote, "If someone says, 'I love God,' and hates his brother, he is a liar" (1 John 4:20). That means if we pray to God and express our love for Him, yet have broken relationships with other people, our words are empty of meaning and our prayer is made void.

The reason we don't have power in our prayer is that God hears more than our words; He hears our life. God sees all, hears all, and knows our innermost thoughts. He isn't fooled by religious rhetoric or well-spoken prayers. When we pray, He hears everything our life is saying.

So what does He hear when *you* pray? What is your life saying to God? When you turn your heart to God in prayer, what do you want Him to hear?

 The power of our prayer is a direct measure of how we abide in Him when we're NOT on our knees.

(Prayer's effectiveness is not the result of what we do when we're praying, but the result of who we *are* when we're *not* praying.) Did you catch that? The power of our prayer doesn't come from our time *in* prayer, but is a direct measure of how we abide in Him when we're *not* on our knees. That's what gives power to our prayer.

PRAYERS THAT ARE HEARD

In the winter of 1971, the doctor told my dad that my mom would die before morning. My dad had just gone to pastor a small struggling church in Canada, and there was little support for him and our family. There were four young boys at home, and Mom had just given birth to a little girl. As a result of many complications, the doctor gave little to no hope that she would survive.

Dad immediately put the word out to others to pray. In particular, he made a phone call to a lady in his previous church in California. It seemed as though when Mrs. Graham prayed, God responded in power.

It was true once more. Something happened that night in eternity, and God saw fit to answer the prayers of His people with the healing of my mom.

Like Mrs. Graham and others, I want to be a person of powerful prayer. I want to be a father who stands before God on behalf of his children. I want to be a pastor who stands before God on behalf of his church. I want to be a man who can boldly come into the throne room of God and intercede on behalf of people in need. And when I do, I want to be heard by Almighty God.

It was the evil Mary Queen of Scots who once said, "I fear John Knox's prayer more than an army of ten thousand men." What is said about *your* prayers? Are you known as a person who prays and sees the power of God move in real life circumstances? When crisis comes, do people think of you as a person they want to pray on their behalf? If not, why not?

Remember His promise: If you abide in Him, and He in you...ask anything you want and it will be done.

There are many victories to be won as you walk with Christ, but they'll come only as you choose to go the second mile in prayer. Let me show you why you need to move beyond the first mile of merely saying grace at mealtime, plus the occasional prayer on the run and bedtime prayers with your children. Your family needs you to go the second mile in prayer, for there may come a time when their life depends on your intercession and the relationship you have with the heavenly Father.

READY TO PRAY FOR THOSE YOU LOVE

My brothers and I were traveling home from a student conference one wintry day in January. It happened to be a Sunday, and Mom was awaiting our arrival later that night. Dad was doing his usual spiritual exercise—the traditional Sunday afternoon nap. Suddenly Mom had an inner compulsion to pray for us. She immediately went to the Lord in prayer, but as she prayed the burden grew stronger. She quickly went to the bedroom and awoke my dad, urging him to pray for us as well. Together, at the side of their bed, they knelt and prayed for our safe return.

We finally arrived home. Mom rushed to give us all hugs, then asked, "What happened today at three o'clock?"

We all had strange looks on our faces. "Why do you ask?"

We understood why we were still alive. For at that exact moment, we needed God's hand of protection.

After she told us of their experience of the Lord's calling them to prayer, we understood why we were still alive. For at that exact moment, we needed God's hand of protection.

We had been going sixty miles an hour down the highway when the driver of our car lost control on a road that was slick with black ice. The car was spinning in circles across the lane of oncoming traffic, and we were headed toward a half-frozen pond on the other side of the highway. Even worse, a semitrailer was approaching for a certain head-on collision. Both options could have been fatal, and there was nothing we could do. We were in the hands of God—or perhaps in the hands of my parents, which at that moment were clasped in prayer for their boys.

Miraculously, at the last possible moment, something caused our car to dart back across to the right and slowly come to a stop in a farmer's field. Coincidence? I think not! We experienced divine intervention because my parents walked with the Lord and had gone the second mile in prayer.

The second mile is about not just you, but also those you love. Your family will be the recipient of your faithfulness to walk with the Lord in prayer. In fact, if you aren't a person of prayer, you've sadly neglected your role as a parent. You're also cheating your friends of a resource that's available to them only through your prayer life.

More than physical protection for your loved ones, eternity is still the great motivator for prayer. There are people all around your life who are lost and have no hope of eternal life with Christ. Remember, there's a spiritual battle going on for the souls of your friends, and you can enter that battle in prayer.

A transformed prayer life is the clearest evidence that a person is walking with Jesus. Remember, God predestined that we become conformed to the image of His Son, and the most characteristic mark of Jesus was His prayer life. To walk on the second mile is to be a person of prayer who impacts eternity.

A HOUSE OF PRAYER

I've been teaching our church to be a house of prayer. I discovered we were good at teaching people the Bible, but not good at teaching people to pray. We fully expected all our members to be involved in Bible study, but we didn't expect them to be involved in a prayer meeting.

Although it was hard to admit, I realized we provided opportunities within the church schedule for every member to be in a Bible study, but we didn't provide an opportunity for every member to be in a prayer meeting. In fact, we had so many scheduled activities at the same time as our prayer meeting that many people couldn't come to pray even if they wanted to. We did have other times when small groups met to pray, but our schedule of activities made it clear that prayer was not a priority.

 The church CAN make a difference, if only we'll go the second mile in prayer.

That has radically changed. We now challenge all members to attend Bible study as well as our Fresh Encounter Prayer Service…and what a difference! There's power in prayer. We've learned that the church *can* make a difference, if only we would go the second mile in prayer.

Not long ago, a lady in our community named Paula was far from God, but anyone who tried to share the gospel with her was immediately shut down. She was adamant that she wanted nothing to do with religion. She'd spent twenty-five years questioning, criticizing, and essentially dismissing Jesus, and she was quite certain her path to God did not lie in Christianity.

But there were people in our church who loved her and were concerned about her eternity. They finally realized that though they couldn't talk to her about Christ, they could talk to Christ about her. They began to pray with great fervency.

Paula is quite an avid hiker and spends time every day walking the trails on her ranch. One particular day not long ago, the Lord met her along the trail. Christ showed Himself to her clearly—with grace, gentleness, and love. In only slightly more than the blink of an eye, all her accumulated skepticism and doubt fell away.

As she told me her story, she said, "I almost feel foolish. For years I told everyone I wanted nothing to do with Jesus, but now all I want to do is follow Him. I know now that Jesus is real and that He's alive and working in my life."

What Paula said at her baptism made me tremble at the

power of answered prayer. It was clear she had a dramatic encounter with the Lord, apart from anything we had done. She said, "After my conversion experience, I thought rather glibly, *Sure, I'm a sinner like anyone else, but really not all that bad of one. I've got my regular, mundane, day-to-day sins, but I haven't committed any really big ones—no murder or adultery.* Well, surprise again. The Holy Spirit revealed to me through a powerful experience that actually I *have* sinned big-time. My sin—my very big sin—was my denial of Jesus. I literally felt the hurt, the heartache, and the sorrow that Jesus felt when I denied Him."

Only God could have impacted Paula with the truth of the gospel. And God chose to work in her life through the prayers of His people. It's still a mystery, but reality nonetheless. Jesus has called us to a life of prayer on the second mile. It can be no other way.

 The kind of prayer that moves heaven requires far more than many are prepared to give.

I could tell story after story of the power in prayer. But the kind of prayer that moves heaven requires far more than many are prepared to give. If we're going to be conformed to the image of God's Son in the area of prayer, we need to look at His prayer life.

The Loud Cries of Jesus

Perhaps the most telling passage of the Lord's prayer life is this one in the book of Hebrews:

> In the days of His flesh, He offered up both prayers and supplications with loud crying and tears to the One able to save Him from death, and He was heard because of His piety. Although He was a Son, He learned obedience from the things which He suffered. And having been made perfect, He became to all those who obey Him the source of eternal salvation. (Hebrews 5:7–9, NASB).

Jesus was flesh and blood, living with the same weaknesses we have today. He got tired; He got hungry; He understood financial poverty; and He felt the struggles we all know so well. He was speaking from personal experience when He told the disciples, "Watch and pray, lest you enter into temptation. The spirit indeed is willing, but the flesh is weak" (Matthew 26:41). He knew the weakness of His flesh and the need for prayer. It was "in the days of His flesh" that He cried out to God in prayer with great passion.

The kind of prayer in Jesus' life wasn't just a quick word at mealtime. This was fervent prayer that resulted in loud crying and tears being offered to the Father. Do those things also characterize *your* prayer life? Are you passionate about calling out to God? Do your prayers well up from within you as a deep longing and crying out to the One who is your life?

It may take some time in His presence to even know what it means to "cry out" to God. It isn't the volume of your voice or the position of your body; crying out is much more significant than that. It's something that comes out of your relationship with Christ when His heart touches your heart.

THE STRUGGLE AND THE VICTORY

In this Hebrews passage, the phrase "although He was a Son" suggests that what we'll read about next is something we wouldn't expect from the Son of God. It's something we wouldn't think Christ would have to endure: Jesus "learned obedience from the things which He suffered." Therein is our problem. We want to have the prayer life of Jesus, but we don't want to struggle. That's why many never experience the kind of prayer life God desires. We haven't gone the second mile in prayer because it costs, and it's demanding of our time.

Our generation says, "I don't want to move out of the comfort zone. I don't want to sacrifice." That's why Jesus said we must deny self, for self will not allow us to experience the prayer life of Jesus. And without going the second mile in prayer, you'll never see the power and influence of being a child of God.

There's an incredible statement in this Hebrews passage

about the outcome of the Lord's prayer life. Through His "piety" (Hebrews 5:7–8, NASB)—also translated as "godly fear" (NKJV), "reverence" (HCSB), or "reverent submission" (NIV)— Jesus was willing to learn obedience by what He suffered. "And having been made perfect, He became to all those who obey Him the source of eternal salvation" (5:9, NASB). Let me briefly apply this statement to you. Do you know that your life becomes a highway over which a lost world comes to the Lord? In prayer, you become an instrument through which God will touch the world.

The Lord said in Ezekiel 22:30–31,

> I searched for a man among them who would build up the wall and stand in the gap before Me for the land, so that I should not destroy it; but I found no one. Thus...I have consumed them with the fire of My wrath. (NASB)

The implication: If just one man had stood before Him in prayer, He would have spared the people.

What happens when you pray?

What happens when you pray? Could you be the one who prays for others so that they receive God's mercy instead of facing God's judgment?

Moses was one who understood this, and he stood before God to plead for his people. God was about to destroy the people because of their sin, so Moses prayed. He stood in the gap before the people, and God heard his prayer and spared them.

Let me ask some serious questions: If the salvation of your neighbors depended on your prayer life, would they stand a chance? If revival in the land depended on your prayer life, would God grant it? If judgment was coming, would your prayers stay the hand of God? If not, then don't complain if God judges the land! If you haven't paid the price in your prayer life, don't complain if things get worse in your community. If you haven't stood before God on behalf of the schools, don't complain if the quality of the school system goes down.

When you look at the prayer life of Jesus, you see that the Father heard Him. Don't underestimate what God could do through *your* life if you would only pray.

Prayer is the contact of a living soul with God. Are there situations in your life that need God's intervention? Are there struggles you cannot overcome? Jesus said, "If you ask anything in My name, I will do it" (John 14:14). Are you being conformed to the image of Christ in your prayer life?

 The Lord is calling you to go the second mile in prayer because He knows your tomorrow.

The reason the Lord is calling you to go the second mile in prayer is that He knows your tomorrow. He knows the needs of your children. He knows your family is about to enter a crisis. He knows your friends don't have much time before eternity comes knocking. Why is He calling you to pray? Because He wants you to be conformed to the image of His Son, and prayer is so deeply a part of that.

THE VIEW FROM THE SECOND MILE: SEEING GOD'S HEART FOR PRAYER

Prayer is the most characteristic mark of Jesus. You can tell those walking with the Lord: They're people of prayer.

But hear this carefully: The state of your prayer life is a reflection not of your faithfulness to perform your Christian duty, but of your faithfulness to God. *Prayer isn't the result of discipline, but the result of a relationship.* I'm not saying discipline and determination aren't important; I'm saying they'll never sustain your prayer life. You'll find that discipline comes and goes; you start off strong, then fade away quickly.

So don't seek a better prayer life; *seek a deeper relationship with Christ.* Like His disciples, ask Him to teach you how to pray. He'll draw you to the place of prayer, and in that place God will hear you. He'll instruct you, and He'll pour Himself into you.

CHAPTER EIGHT

ABUNDANT LIVING

Seeing God's Blessing

I have come that they may have life,
and that they may have it more abundantly.
John 10:10

Have you ever been to a restaurant where they don't have free refills on drinks? When that's the case, how do you consume your drink?

That may sound like a trivial question, but there are times when this has made a big difference in my life.

My wife and I were on a mission trip to Africa and had to be careful about what we ate or drank. To consume some "bad water" would mean a bad time for our delicate North American systems. One evening Gina and I found ourselves at a primitive restaurant where we weren't comfortable with the quality of hygiene, so we were careful not to drink the water or eat anything washed in water. To quench our thirst, we each had a bottle of pop.

Back to my original question: How do you consume your drink? Gina and I approach such a decision very differently. I budget; she downs it! That is, I make sure to sip my drink in such a way that it will last the entire meal. I don't want to be out of drink too early and end up with a dry mouth and without the means to wash something down at the end of the meal. My wife, on the other hand, thinks differently: *If it's good, why wait?*

So there we were, halfway through the meal, and Gina was looking longingly at my half-full bottle because hers was already empty. I had been trying to pace myself, while she had run dry…and I wish I could say it was easy for me to go "the second mile" and share! Out of love for my wife, however, I sacrificed.

SATISFYING REFRESHMENT

Imagine being in a hot place. Dust is in the air, your mouth is dry, your lips are chapped, and you're desperate for something to drink. You see a cooler with a glass front, filled with rows of ice-cold drinks. You stumble across the room to take a drink, but discover the door is locked. There's no way to get in! Refreshment is only inches away, yet out of your reach. Those drinks are right there, but they may as well be a million miles away.

When it comes to your soul's thirst, do you know how to find refreshment? Are you experiencing abundant life? Or does it seem to be just out of your reach?

Jesus said, "I have come that they may have life, and that they may have it more abundantly" (John 10:10). Jesus promised that those who follow Him will always be satisfied. Those who deny self, pick up their cross, and follow Him will experience abundant life.

Listen to some of the images Jesus gave us to describe a satisfying relationship with Himself:

But whoever drinks of the water that I shall give him will never thirst. But the water that I shall give him will become in him a fountain of water springing up into everlasting life. (John 4:14)

I am the bread of life. He who comes to Me shall never hunger. (John 6:35)

I am the light of the world. He who follows Me shall not walk in darkness, but have the light of life. (John 8:12)

I am the good shepherd. The good shepherd gives His life for the sheep. (John 10:11)

You get the sense that Jesus is using every expression possible to communicate love and care for His people. He's the *living water* that quenches our thirst, the *bread* that satisfies our hunger, the *light* that brings us out of darkness, the *shepherd* who protects us. In other words, a relationship with Christ *satisfies.*

So let me ask a simple question: Are you satisfied? Do you feel empty? Perhaps you took it all in and it tasted so good at salvation, but suddenly it's gone and you're all dried up.

Somewhere along the way it all began to seem too routine. The joy of salvation is no longer there.

Or maybe you're one who has tried to "budget"? You've paced yourself and worked hard to do the right thing, but somewhere along the way it all began to seem too routine. The joy of salvation is no longer there. The promise Jesus made to give us "rivers of living water" (John 7:38) sounds so good— but seems so far away.

ABUNDANT GIVING, ABUNDANT LIVING

So where do I find abundant life?

Listen to the clearest statement of discipleship in the Bible: "If anyone desires to come after Me, let him deny himself, and take up his cross, and follow Me. For whoever desires to save his life will lose it, but whoever loses his life for My sake will find it" (Matthew 16:24–25). abundant life ≠ monetary

Jesus is saying, "Deny self…and *you'll have abundant life.* Pick up your cross…and *you'll have abundant life.* Follow Me… and *you'll have abundant life.* Lose your life for My sake…and *you'll have abundant life."* The reality of the second mile is that there's a cost to following Christ and to experiencing the abundant life He offers—and there is sacrifice that's unavoidable.

(Listen carefully: *Abundant life is found in abundant living.*) We tend to have a self-centered view of abundant life. That is, we think in terms of what we *receive,* not what we *give.* When Jesus said, "I have come to give abundant life," we respond, "Bring it on! I want love…give me love more abundantly. I want joy…give me joy more abundantly. I want peace…give me peace more abundantly. I want blessings from God…give me blessing more abundantly." On and on we go, dreaming of all that God will give us.

We want abundant life, but we aren't sure about denying self, picking up a cross, and following Jesus. We want abundant life, but we aren't sure we want to give our life away. We fail to realize that receiving abundant life is found on the other side of giving our life away for the sake of Christ. There's a divine interplay between our giving and our receiving.)

Not that we give in order to receive, as though we could earn God's blessing. Remember again what Jesus said: "Give, and it will be given to you: good measure, pressed down, shaken together, and running over will be put into your bosom. For with the same measure that you use, it will be measured back to you" (Luke 6:38). Don't wait for abundant life...*live it!*

FROM SACRIFICE TO BLESSING

I'll never forget serving in a small church as pastor right out of seminary. My wife and I had just had our first child, we were flat broke after several years of school, and I was the only person on staff. Although we approached the situation like a church plant, technically it was a "restart," and the situation was bleak. It was an old church that was all but dead. The people were discouraged, numbers were small, the building was decrepit, resources were very limited, and the reputation of the church in the community wasn't good.

But while others had given up on it, the Lord still cared about His people in that place and was sending us to lay down our lives for them. As we approached this assignment, the Lord said to us, "Mission work is hard...but will you still go? I love those people, and I have a purpose for that church."

We knew if we stepped out in faith, God would be faithful.

We *did* go, and it *was* hard. But we knew if we stepped out in faith, God would be faithful.

I remember making a conscious decision to sacrifice for the Lord. I listed all the things I was going to give up in order to go to this church. While in seminary, I was the pastor of a church that was growing, reaching the lost, and full of loving people who cared for my family. In our minds, we were walking away from a great place and stepping into a very difficult one. But that was okay. The Lord Jesus had given up much to leave the throne room of God and come to earth for our salvation, and we were excited to sacrifice for Him.

But as we gave our lives for the church in this new assignment from God, He seemed just to give right back. In fact, those first few years were some of the greatest years of ministry we've ever known, for we saw the Lord working at every step we took. As we gave to the Lord, He gave back abundantly.

One of the greatest blessings became people who partnered with us. That little church building desperately needed a face-lift. So we painted the outside, landscaped the property, completely renovated the inside, and even changed the church's name. But we were a small group with no money and needed help to accomplish all that. That's when a church in Tennessee sent twenty-one people to help us. We were in the middle of tearing out the old rooms and building new ones. The work was demanding, but I'd never seen a group work so hard and so long.

I began to feel a little guilty about their spending all their time in hard labor, so I suggested they take at least one evening off to see the sights. A few of the ladies in the grouped decided to shop for souvenirs, but all the men said, "We would like to use our free time working on the church. Can we keep working?"

I couldn't believe it. They had traveled from Tennessee to Canada and were spending all their time in a dusty old building hanging sheetrock. I tried to talk them into taking time off (partly because I, too, had to keep working as long as they were on the job). But they insisted. This group laid down their lives for us, and we made huge forward strides on the project.

Only the love of God could compel people to make such sacrifice.

The Lord allowed me to see two amazing things about the second mile during that week. The first happened through a man who had been coming to our church only a short time and who was still checking us out. He was a big, gruff mechanic who owned a radiator shop. As he watched the church crew working all week, he came to me in absolute amazement. Moved with emotion he asked, "Why are these people doing this? They've spent a lot of money getting here and worked like crazy the whole time—and they don't even know us!" He couldn't get over it. For him, this was the greatest gospel witness ever; only the love of God could compel people to make such sacrifice. He was forever changed as a recipient of service on the second mile.

The other significant moment was with one of the men

on that team. I discovered he had only one week of vacation for the year, and he was taking it for this trip. He'd never really traveled before, let alone been to Canada. When he heard about the mission trip, he desperately wanted to go but couldn't afford it. So his Sunday school class took a love offering and paid for his plane fare.

Once he arrived, he was one of the hardest workers on the team. And as they were about to leave, he came up to me with tears rolling down his cheeks and said, "Thank you so much for letting me come. I can't express how much God has blessed my life by being here with you this week." I was stunned. He was thanking *me?* But it was obvious he'd been on the second mile, and the Lord was measuring back into his life more than he had given.

The Source of Abundance

At the time of your salvation, God gave you the Holy Spirit so you could love more abundantly, give more abundantly, forgive more abundantly, show kindness more abundantly, and serve the Lord with power from on high. And when you give away what you've received from Him, He just keeps filling you up. The more you "live abundantly," the more you receive abundant life from God.

That's what Jesus was talking about when He told us to

deny self, pick up our cross, and follow Him. It's in following Jesus—allowing Him to live out His purposes in you—that you know the joy of the Lord.

God's children have the opportunity to experience incredible blessings of God. Yet God has chosen to work His blessings in our lives in proportion to how we receive them—how we allow them to change our hearts.

The Bible is clear at this point. We aren't a holding tank of blessings, but a channel. We must acknowledge His blessing by sharing it with others.

Remember again the Lord's promise: "I have come that they may have life, and that they may have it more abundantly" (John 10:10). If you're wondering why you aren't experiencing abundant life as Jesus promised, it may be for this very reason: You don't have a thankful heart that passes on His blessings to those around you. You don't look to bless others, even though God has blessed you. You aren't sensitive to others, even though God cares so deeply for you. You will not forgive others, even though God forgave you. You long to have God pour out blessings in your life, but you're unwilling to do the same for others.

Those who are on the second mile have a generous heart like Christ's.

Those who are on the second mile have a generous heart like Christ's. And His promise to those who walk the second mile is clear: As you have measured, it will be measured back to you.

When the apostle Peter told Jesus, "See, we have left all and followed You," Jesus replied,

> Assuredly, I say to you, there is no one who has left house or parents or brothers or wife or children, for the sake of the kingdom of God, who shall not receive many times more *in this present time*, and *in the age to come* eternal life. (Luke 18:29–30)

What He was saying is simply this: "Don't you know that if you give what little you have for the sake of the kingdom of God, the God of the universe who owns it all will also freely give to you? Don't you realize that those with generous hearts who give to God will also come to know His generous heart toward their own life? You cannot outgive God! Your gifts will never equal what He gives back to the generous heart."

The second mile is a natural response to a thankful heart. So after all God has done for you, how have you responded to Him? Does He expect to see fruit in your life as a result of the blessings He bestows? Absolutely. Grace calls for a response.

A STORY OF ABUNDANCE

When you live abundantly, you'll also find that God brings people into your life who will abundantly bless you and your family as well. I have a good friend, Bob, who found himself in a situation he never dreamed he would be in. He was checked into the hospital in critical condition, not knowing if he would live through the experience. He had many complications, but at the center of his problem was his pancreas.

As his life was hanging by a thread, he experienced a verse in Scripture that became very meaningful: "For the despairing man there should be kindness from his friend" (Job 6:14, NASB). His Sunday school class at church walked the second mile and surrounded Bob and his family with kindness.

It was comforting to know somebody cared, and that he could count on his friend.

In the first hospital he was in, one of the doctors there happened to be one of his close friends at church. He would come every morning at six o'clock to hold his hand and talk with him. It just so happened that Bob's most painful times of the day were always between 3:00 and 6:00 a.m., and he came to look forward to seeing his friend stop by to help him endure the pain. It was comforting to know that somebody cared and that he could count on his friend.

As the days turned into months, the needs in Bob's family began to grow. His doctor friend plus another person in Bob's Sunday school class came to Bob's home every Wednesday for eight months to cut his grass and take care of his yard.

Time in the hospital began to wear Bob out; it just seemed like the pain would never end. But his friends kept coming to sit with him and carry his burden. On one particular day, he'd just gone through a trying procedure and the pain was so great he couldn't stop crying. As he was wheeled back into his room, his wife also was moved to tears, not knowing how to help her husband. At a moment when the pain intensified and Bob was afraid, another friend from church walked into his room. He was a seventy-five-year-old third-generation missionary to Brazil with a voice as deep as the Grand Canyon. He too held Bob's hand, smiled, and began to quote the book of Psalms verse by verse. Immediately, there was peace in the room.

Life had to go on, but Bob and his wife couldn't keep up. It was at this time that another family in the church stepped in to care for what was most precious to them; they took in their fourteen-year-old son Douglas for nine months. The family of God cared for Bob's family over and above what he'd expected.

Bob underwent many procedures, but nothing seemed to help. Finally he was sent to a large medical center where an acclaimed surgeon told him his only chance was to remove all or part of his pancreas. Bob was told he wouldn't survive without the surgery, and there was only a 30 percent survival rate even if it was successful. The procedure would leave him with various limitations, but at least he would be alive.

As he prepared to undergo surgery, Bob asked the surgeon to listen to his favorite CD, "Experiencing God Musical," while he performed the operation. The doctor agreed.

Three days later Bob awoke to news from the doctor that the pancreas had *not* been removed, and Bob immediately was devastated. He was overcome with grief at the thought of leaving his family after months of fighting. The physical pain he'd endured was unbelievable, but even more, it hurt to watch his family suffer emotionally and financially through this time.

> He felt he had the power to do something different than he'd ever done before.

The surgeon, however, had much more to tell Bob. He related how just three days before the procedure, he'd received several handwritten prayer cards from people at Bob's church who said they would be in prayer for the doctor until the operation was over. Then he added, "While I was in surgery, I felt as though I had the *power* to do something different than I'd ever done before." He did, and it saved Bob's life!

During recovery, Bob was given temporary passes out of the hospital so he could go home for the weekends. On one particular Saturday, he awoke to the sound of forty men and several women from his church who showed up at 7:00 a.m. They'd discovered that his house needed repairs that Bob couldn't afford. They painted his home's exterior, installed new window shutters, landscaped the yard, and built a small park area that would later become a prayer garden for Bob and his grandson. While they worked, they also found two holes in the roof and took care of that problem the same day. They worked with all their might until 8:00 p.m., doing whatever was necessary to take care of the home.

During their lunch break, the group gathered on the driveway to have a bite to eat. Bob convinced his wife to wheel him out front so he could thank his friends. So they gathered up all the various medical devices attached to his body, and they took him out to the driveway. As best he could manage, he thanked them with words that seemed so insufficient.

Then Bob realized one of the men was still working atop a high ladder around back. So he found his way to the back deck where he could talk with his friend. Through tears Bob began to express his thanks for all the man was doing for him and his family: "I don't know how to thank you; I don't have the words…" At that point his friend looked down from the ladder and tears began to roll down his cheeks. "Bob," he said, "you don't have to say a thing. *This is the happiest day of my life!*"

THE VIEW FROM THE SECOND MILE:
SEEING GOD'S BLESSING

God has a law of identical harvest: "Whatever a man sows, that he will also reap" (Galatians 6:7). Believers operate in a covenant relationship with God. We often talk about God's "unconditional love" when we talk of God's relationship toward His children. I believe in God's unconditional love, but the Bible never talks about "unconditional blessing." God loves His children no matter what they do, but the same isn't true with blessings. The measure with which we use is measured back to us. Abundant life is experienced in direct correlation to how we live it. Do you live abundantly? Do you give to others freely and generously?

If God were to give to you in the same measure you give to others, what could you expect from heaven? If He were to forgive in the same measure you have forgiven, how would you stand before God? If He were to show kindness in the same measure you show kindness to those in your life, what would you experience in life?

Make sure you understand this kingdom principle: "With the measure you use, it will be measured back to you" (Matthew 7:2).

Don't wait for abundant life...*live it now* on the second mile.

A PARABLE OF THE SECOND MILE

Seeing a Life Well Spent

Well done, good and faithful servant…
Enter into the joy of your lord.
Matthew 25:21

The second mile continually leads into places you've never been…and into an existence that's far beyond anything you could experience on your own.

It's like a man who worked hard all his life, gave his very best at everything he attempted, fulfilled his duty as expected, and was known for being a good person.

But as he walked along the road, he met the man called Jesus Christ. Jesus called out to him and said, "You've walked the first mile of your life very well. Your colleagues speak highly of you, and your family adores you. The world admires the efforts of a job well done.

"But there's much more to life than doing your best; you can experience *God's* best. You have a good life—but if you want *abundant* life, you must walk with Me on the second mile.

"If you're willing, I'll take you to places of such abundance that the world will marvel...and the heavenly Father will smile.

"Will you walk with Me on the second mile?"

How do I get to the second mile?

The invitation was intriguing. And the sound of Jesus' voice was assuring. The man always knew there was something more to life than he'd known, but he had no idea what it was or how to get there. "The second mile?" he inquired of Jesus. "How do I get to the second mile?"

"Simple," Jesus replied. "Just come to Me, take My hand, and I'll teach you. I've been on the second mile a long time; on that road I've experienced life as the Father intended, and I'll share it with you. If you choose to walk with Me, I'll give you My joy. But before you come—you need to know there's no turning back."

The look in Jesus' eye was enough to convince the man he

wanted the joy of the Lord no matter the cost. So he took one small step toward Jesus…and immediately felt the hand of the Lord take hold of him.

A sudden rush of joy flooded his life—an indescribable peace and contentment. Who could have known?

By now he was convinced Jesus would satisfy the emptiness he'd always felt. He told himself, *Turn back from this? You've got to be kidding!*

"Just remember," Jesus reminded the man, "you must stay close to Me. You must learn to recognize My voice. There'll be times when we go through a valley, when the shadows may distort reality. It's then that you need to recognize My voice and respond to My directions in the darkness."

A TIME TO FORGIVE

Those early days were special. The man came to understand just how deeply the Lord loved him. It was as though nothing else mattered, for His love had no end. His love relationship with Christ was more than he ever imagined and certainly more than he ever deserved.

It was no trouble to stay on the road, for there was nowhere else he would rather be.

One day Jesus took him along a path that seemed familiar. This path, however, wasn't where the man wanted to go; in fact, it triggered memories of pain and sorrow. It was an old friend who had brought great heartache. And there the friend was—as full of pride and arrogance as he'd always been! Just the sight of him aroused anxiety and caused the man to turn away.

"Do you remember this man?" Jesus said.

"How could I forget?"

"Forgive him," Jesus commanded.

"But Lord! You don't know what he did. You don't know how I've been treated. You don't understand how difficult it is for me to forgive *this* man!"

While the man pleaded his case, Jesus' countenance was somehow strangely different—almost as if He also was remembering some distant pain in His life.

Quietly Jesus responded, "I do understand. I've been there. I know the pain of betrayal. You're going to have to trust Me on this one. *Forgive him.*"

There's no turning back. But you can't go forward until you forgive.

The man began to squirm and turn away, but the hand of Jesus wouldn't let him go. "Remember," Jesus said, "there's no turning back. But we can't go forward until you forgive. If you don't forgive this man, you'll spend the rest of your life with bitterness in your heart, and the past will have such a grip on your life that you won't see clearly to follow Me."

He knew Jesus was right, and he didn't want to miss out

on the rest of the journey with his Lord. But taking this step of forgiveness was so difficult!

Breaking the awkward silence, Jesus reassured him: "It's okay. Just forgive him…and you'll be free."

Jesus was right! The moment the man forgave his estranged friend, it felt as if a ton of bricks were lifted off his heart. Unforgiveness had been a weight he didn't even know he was carrying. But not anymore—now he had energy to walk with Christ with even greater speed.

A Time to Bless

The man realized he still had a lot to learn about the second mile, but Jesus was faithful to teach him how to walk with renewed strength.

But as they continued walking, Jesus brought him back to the same former friend once more. This time, Jesus quietly whispered, "Bless him."

"Lord! I already forgave him. What more do You want from me?"

"I want you to bless him," Jesus said again.

"But Lord, You don't know what He said about me. He openly cursed me before others!"

"I understand," Jesus said. "On the second mile, you must bless those who curse you and desire their good."

The man realized that the further they traveled along the second mile, the more foreign this pathway seemed. Still grappling with the lesson before him, he heard the Savior's voice of experience say, "My best friend cursed My name at a time when I needed him the most…and it hurt. Bless him."

It took a few more moments of talking with Jesus, but eventually the man saw his old friend differently. He saw him through the eyes of the Lord and realized his friend desperately needed someone to speak a word of encouragement.

After Jesus gave him the right words to say, he proceeded to share them with his friend.

He realized he had power to bring joy into another's life.

Forgiving his friend had brought immediate joy in the heart of the man, but blessing his friend brought something much different. The man now realized he had power to bring joy into another person's life. His concern wasn't just for his own life anymore; now he wanted his friend to know the joy of the Lord. Who knew that words had such power?

"On the second mile," Jesus explained, "take time to speak words that will heal. It isn't hard, if only you'll choose to do it."

A TIME TO DO GOOD

They didn't walk far before they stopped again—and once more, the man's old friend was there.

This time Jesus commanded, "Do good to him."

"But Lord," the man protested, "I have a busy life and my time is precious. I would rather spend my time doing good to those who appreciate me, not to those who don't care about me. I've forgiven him, I've offered him words of encouragement, but to give my time and effort to do him good—I just don't know if I can do it."

This was so unlike any road the man had ever been on. He'd always been a good person, but nobody ever expected him to do this—to go this far. The second mile was like nothing he'd ever known.

Once more he heard the Lord speak, this time with a slight tremble in His voice: "I know it's hard to do good to those who hate you and to pray for those who spitefully use you. I understand what you're feeling. I had a trusted friend who used Me, who handed Me over to evil men for money of little value. The Father asked Me to kneel before this man—and wash his feet. So believe Me when I say I understand."

The man realized in a fresh way how he'd come to love and trust Jesus; He seemed to know what He was talking about.

Again Jesus gave the command: "Do good to him."

So the man did good to his old friend. The hardest part,

however, wasn't doing good, but *choosing* to do good. Once the decision was made, something inside took over, and the action of serving brought great joy. For with every good deed he attempted, he was reminded of all the good the Lord had done for him.

In a way, it became his way of thanking the Lord for all the good he'd received without deserving it. The man came to understand that on the second mile, a good deed isn't done because people deserve it, but because *you* are good. It's the nature of the giver, not the receiver, which determines action on the second mile.

Although this was the most difficult lesson to learn on the second mile thus far, it also brought the deepest joy. More than ever, the man felt the pleasure of God.

A TIME TO GIVE ALL

Jesus, however, wasn't through. He turned to the man once more. "Lay down your life," He said.

"My *life?* Lord, that's all I have left!"

"That's why you must give it," Jesus replied. "Die to self that you might live for Me. That's the last step in the second mile, and it yields the true meaning of abundant life on earth. For no one has greater love than this—to lay down his life for his friends."

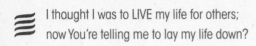

I thought I was to LIVE my life for others;
now You're telling me to lay my life down?

The man was confused. "I thought I was to *live* my life to help others; now You're telling me to lay my life down?"

"I know it doesn't make sense," Jesus replied. "But it's true. The kingdom of God is much different from the world you've known. In My Father's kingdom, the first will be last, and the last will be first. In His kingdom, you'll lose your life if you try to save it, but you'll find your life if you give it away for My sake. In His kingdom, you must die to self that you might have abundant life in Christ. I know what I'm talking about—it was through My death on the cross that I experienced resurrection power and secured eternal life to all who would believe.

"It isn't what you do for the Father, but what the Father does *in* you that matters. Trust Me; lay down your life, and the Father will raise you up."

The man was in a place he never thought existed. He'd always been told to affirm self, to build his self-esteem. Now Jesus was telling him to deny self, even die to self. It made no sense.

But he'd come this far, and the Lord had proven again and again to be faithful and true.

The man turned to Jesus. With tears in his eyes, he said, "I don't know what to do. I don't know how to fully give You my life…so take *me*. I'm Yours."

With a willing heart and an open life, he allowed the Lord

to take his dreams and replace them with the Father's will…to take his human strategies for service and replace them with kingdom ways…to take his growing reputation and replace it with the glory of God. The man's life was no longer his own; it belonged to Another.

And now…in a strange way…life on the second mile was no longer a burden. It was no longer difficult to sacrifice for others; life was no longer full of stress and anxiety. For his life was no longer his to give. Christ was in charge, and the man knew that whatever Christ chose to do, He was fully capable of doing.

All the power of God was now displayed through the man's life. And what a life it was! The joy of walking with Christ surpassed any previous expectation.

AT THE FINAL GATE

As they walked through life on the second mile, the man suddenly realized that the road was coming to an end. He turned and saw Jesus by his side as they approached a gate. Amid the brilliance of the moment, everything seemed so right. The road he'd been walking was worth it—every step along the way.

He realized Jesus had taken him far beyond himself to a destination he could never have reached on his own—the second mile led him *right to the throne room of God!*

Looking up into the face of God, the man heard the most

unusual words: "Welcome home, My son! Enter into your rest." And he realized for the first time that he'd been conformed to the image of God's Son…on the second mile.

The View from the Second Mile: Seeing a Life Well Spent

Heaven awaits the believer, and it's a place beyond human words to describe. But one thing we know for certain: Heaven is good. The biblical writers used words to describe the best place they could imagine, though I have a sense it will be far beyond what we can comprehend.

The rewards we receive in heaven are in God's hands, but that doesn't mean we don't have the opportunity now, in this life, to impact our time in eternity. Jesus said,

> Do not lay up for yourselves treasures on earth, where moth and rust destroy and where thieves break in and steal; but *lay up for yourselves treasures in heaven,* where neither moth nor rust destroys and where thieves do not break in and steal. (Matthew 6:19–20)

The life we live on earth impacts eternity. Christ will return someday and "reward each according to his works" (Matthew 16:27).

To walk the second mile means seeing things from eternity's perspective, where the view of what's important becomes abundantly clear: People are worth the investment, for people will live forever—some in the presence of God, and some separated from Him. The Lord desires to bring into His kingdom as many people as will receive Him. And you and I are the instruments through which He will do it.

There are people all around your life who are lonely and hurting. There are people who are buried up to their eyes in sin and don't know how to get free. There are people who are lost and without hope...and eternity is looming.

Heaven and its rewards await the believer, so don't resist sacrifice. Everything you do is seen; everything will be accounted for. Take that step toward Jesus, and walk with Him on the second mile.

MILE MARKERS

Questions for Your Reflection
& Application

AFTER YOU'VE READ CHAPTER 1 — "THE ROAD LESS TRAVELED: *SEEING OUR NEED*"

1. What are your hopes and expectations about what you'll learn from reading this book?

2. In this book's title, what does that phrase *the second mile* mean to you?

3. Have you ever had one of those days when you don't feel appreciated for all the good things you do? If so, what brought about this feeling?

4. How well can you relate with this story about helping a friend with a broken–down car?

5. How often do you forget how much God has done for you?

6. Think about the events that have shaped your life, the people who've invested in you, and the good things you've experienced. In what ways do you see God's hand in these things?

7. How obvious has God's presence been in your life?

Compelled by Love

8. When you serve others, what is your motivation? How often are you motivated by the recognition you hope to receive from others?

9. How often is your service to others motivated by your appreciation of God's love and blessings for you?

10. How fully do you realize that everything God has done for you, He did not *have* to do?

The Smile of Christ

11. In general, do you consider yourself to be someone who is sacrificial, ready to do whatever it takes to follow the Lord?

12. Of the Christians you know, which ones show the most evidence of living the abundant life Christ promised? Which ones seem full of the joy of the Lord?

Sacrifice

13. What stands out to you most in this brief account of Lavish, the African pastor?

14. As you think about the concept of "the second mile," what questions do you have? What do you want to learn about this?

Second-Mile Study

For your further exploration and reflection in God's Word— look up 2 Corinthians 8:9. What has the love of Christ done for you?

AFTER YOU'VE READ CHAPTER 2 —
"BEYOND DUTY:
SEEING GOD'S LOVE"

1. Read carefully through the words of Jesus in Matthew 5:38–45, either in your own Bible or as reprinted in this book at the beginning of Chapter 2. Seriously consider what the Lord is saying to you through this passage. What is Christ commanding you to do?

A Familiar Picture

2. The second mile is where we find the Lord doing His work. Where do you see Him at work today?

3. Imagine yourself as a Jew living in Roman-occupied Israel at the time of Jesus, where any day a Roman soldier might demand that you carry his load for one mile. How would you respond to Christ's command to also go a second mile?

4. How does this command of Jesus go beyond the concept of "duty"?

5. *Why* are we to love our enemies…and bless those who curse us…and do good to those who hate us…and pray for those who spitefully use us and persecute us?

6. In what ways have you been guilty of wanting a "second helping" of the Lord's blessings more than you've wanted to walk the second mile with Him?

7. What evidence do you see in your own life of a worldly desire to seek your own ease and to follow the path of least resistance?

From the Heart

8. When it comes to serving God, have you ever seen someone do the right thing for the wrong reasons? In what ways have you ever done this yourself?

9. The Lord's foremost desire is to have us *be* right rather than to *do* right. Why is this true?

Gratefully Sharing Our Blessings

10. How easy is it for you to share with others the things which you have received as a gift?

11. Why is it wrong to hoard for yourself the blessings you receive? What harm does this bring?

The Driving Force

12. Do you understand how generous God has been toward you? How thankful are you for this?

13. Knowing how much God has done in your own life, how have you received His gifts? How much have you given back to Him?

Throughout the Bible

14. Consider carefully what the Lord is saying to you through each of the passages referred to in this section. Think about your response to each one:
    —Matthew 5:43–45 (loving your enemies)
    —Philippians 2:4 (looking out for others' interests)
    —Luke 10:30–35 (the story of the Good Samaritan)
    —John 6:60–68 (staying with Jesus when others fall away)
    —1 Thessalonians 2:8–9 (imparting your own life in ministry labor)
    —2 Corinthians 8:3 (giving financially beyond your ability)

The View from the Second Mile: Seeing God's Love

15. In what ways have you been satisfied in your life to do what any "good person" would do? How satisfied have you been with simply a job well done?

16. In your life, do others see what *you* have accomplished—and nothing more?

17. Can other people see Christ in your life?

Second-Mile Study

For your further exploration and reflection in God's Word—study 2 Peter 1:3–11 to see what the Lord has provided to equip you for the second mile.

AFTER YOU'VE READ CHAPTER 3—
"MORE THAN A GOOD PERSON:
SEEING GOD'S PURPOSE"

1. Who have been the best neighbors you've ever known?

Second-Mile Neighbors

2. In your relationships with those who live near you, how have you been able to go above and beyond what's expected of a good neighbor?

3. Together with others in your church, are you finding ways to show the love of Christ to your neighbors?

4. In your church, who are the most generous and kind people?

Beyond Good

5. What has God called you to do that is supernatural, something that cannot be done in your own strength?

6. What has God called you to do that makes no sense to human reasoning?

7. How does your own life reflect an understanding of what is eternally valuable?

8. How do you see Christ displaying His life through other believers you know? And how is He displaying His life through *you?*

The World Sees Christ

9. Why is it impossible to simply imitate the nature of Christ?

10. What is the Lord's standard for how you treat other people?

11. What has convinced you of the impossibility of sustaining Christlike attitudes and actions through your own strength and determination?

12. When it comes to how we relate to others, what is the real difference between Christ's way and the world's way?

13. What is the difference between being Christ-controlled and self-controlled?

14. How has your life been marked by doing the unexpected—by doing what isn't normal for people to do, so that you reflect the nature of God?

Fighting Evil with Good

15. How does your life indicate a priority for eternal things?

16. In your life today, how can you fight evil with good?

17. In your own life today, how can you be generous in a situation where you don't have to be?

18. In your own life today, how can you freely show forgiveness?

19. In your own life today, how can you show kindness and gentleness?

20. In your own life today, how can you give your best and do more than is expected?

21. In your own life today, how can you live with integrity?

22. In your own life today, how can you help God's people by giving generously, serving willingly, and laying down your life for the Lord's sake?

Only Getting By?

23. In your own life, how have you experienced godly sorrow that leads to repentance? Is there a need for such repentance now in your life?

24. In what ways, if any, have you been guilty of seeking to do only the minimum requirements of Christianity?

25. In what ways are you perhaps too casual in your attitude toward the Lord?

From a Right Heart

26. In your own life, how have you seen the impossibility of "outgiving God"?

27. How have you discovered personally that when you give your life away, you find it?

28. What does it mean to you that God rewards your heart, not your duty?

29. Why is having the right heart before God so important in doing what we do to serve others?

Ready, Aim, Fire

30. Consider how much time you have spent learning and getting ready for Christian service. Have you fully put that training into action?

31. Where do you see the Lord at work *now?* Are you there with Him? Are you walking with Him *now?*

The View from the Second Mile: Seeing God's Purpose

32. Are you where Christ is, and doing what *He* is doing?

33. Right now, what does it mean to be living your life on God's terms?

34. Ponder again these questions: When people see your life, what do they see? *Who* do they see? What is Jesus doing through your life?

Second-Mile Study

For your further exploration and reflection in God's Word—consider God's purpose for your life as you study Matthew 7:15–23.

AFTER YOU'VE READ CHAPTER 4— "BREAKING THE ONE-MILE BARRIER: *SEEING GOD'S INVITATION*"

1. In what ways do you tend to be self-reliant? Are you smart enough to know when you truly need help?

Letting Jesus Take Over

2. What does it mean to you that walking the second mile is more about *relationship* than it is about activity?

3. Have you given your life *completely* to Christ?

4. Read carefully through the words of Jesus in Matthew 11:25–30, either in your own Bible or as reprinted in this book near the beginning of Chapter 4. Seriously consider what the Lord is saying in this passage. What is Christ inviting you to do?

5. Do you tend to be a person who "has it all figured out," or in a childlike way do you recognize your need?

6. How have you seen that those who are "wise in the world" end up being crippled by their so-called knowledge?

7. Why does calling for God's help require humility?

8. How fully do you realize that there's much you don't know, and that the knowledge you do possess is not final?

The First Requirement

9. How have you actually *come* to Jesus? What has this meant in your life? What does it mean for you today?

10. What is on the Lord's heart today? Have you come close enough to Him to find out?

11. Have you ever come to the Lord for merely a "quick fix"? How does He truly want you to come to Him? What does He want you to come *for*?

12. If the two classes of humanity are the willing and the unwilling...in which category are you?

13. Are you someone who likes to be in charge? Do you feel that's how you were made?

What Is Faith?

14. What wrong ideas about faith have you had?

15. What really is faith?

16. Right now, in what ways does God want you to rearrange your life and make necessary adjustments in order to obey His will?

17. In order to experience God's mighty power in your life, what is it likely to cost you?

Answer Yes

18. Have you already given your unqualified "Yes" to God for whatever He will want from you or ask of you? Can you genuinely say, "Lord, whatever You ask me to do, the answer is yes"?

19. Are there some things God might ask of you (or *is* asking of you) that you find yourself unwilling to do? If so, what are these things? How does God want you to deal with this?

No Hesitation

20. What reservations do you have about fully coming to Christ, ready to obey whatever He requires of you?

21. How is your life today a true reflection of your faith?

22. Are you consistently listening to God, believing Him, responding to Him, and seeing His glory in your life as you live according to His will?

No Doubt

23. Why is it that so many Christians do *not* walk the second mile? Why do so many fail to do what they must in order to see the mighty power of God in their lives?

24. In what ways, if any, have you been guilty of doubting God?

25. Think about whatever tough circumstances you may be experiencing at this time, or whatever criticism you may be hearing from others. In the face of these things, are your eyes firmly fixed on Christ? Are your ears listening to His voice?

No Fear

26. As you think about how truly you want to live with significance and purpose, and how genuinely you wish to please the Lord, what fears can get in the way of experiencing this?

27. How have you seen the Lord at work to dissipate your fears?

28. How is God allowing you to "lay hold on eternal things," as A. W. Tozer prayed? How is God working in your heart to make heaven "more real…than any earthly thing has ever been"?

The View from the Second Mile: Seeing God's Invitation

29. In the Lord's presence, and by His Spirit, allow yourself to put aside worldly distractions and advice and to look into the face of Jesus. Do you trust Him? Do you believe He loves you? Are you convinced He'll give you abundant life?

30. Do you hear Jesus saying to you, "Come"? If so…what will be your answer?

Second-Mile Study

For your further reflection in God's Word—evaluate your faith in light of Hebrews 11:1, 11:6, and 12:1–2.

AFTER YOU'VE READ CHAPTER 5—
"IN STEP WITH CHRIST:
SEEING GOD'S STRENGTH"

1. Think about the life of your Lord and Savior, Jesus Christ. What was "narrow" and difficult about the "road" He walked?

2. What is difficult about the road the Lord wants you to walk?

3. What specific courage and comfort do you find in the fact that you need never walk alone…that you're to walk *with Christ?*

4. Think about what "following Christ" means to you. That word *follow* implies movement, change, and perhaps new directions—and it always means forward progress. How are you seeing movement, change, and forward progress in your life?

5. In what ways, if any, is there stagnation in your life?

It Isn't Easy

6. How would you respond to a nonbeliever who tells you he is afraid of going to hell?

7. How would you respond to a nonbeliever who tells you she is overwhelmed with anxiety and stress?

8. How would you respond to a nonbeliever who tells you he is facing a great challenge that he does not feel prepared for?

9. How would you respond to an elderly nonbeliever who tells you she is afraid of dying?

10. In the situations mentioned in the four previous questions, what would you say about a *relationship* with Christ?

11. In what ways have you expected that following Jesus as your Lord should mean greater ease in your life, and the taking away of hardships?

Take His Yoke

12. What does Jesus want you to *take* from Him?

13. What does the "yoke" of Jesus mean to you? What pic-

tures does it bring to mind? As the Lord invites you to take His yoke upon you, how do you understand this?

14. In a time of difficulty, have you ever told God, "I don't know how much more of this I can take"? If so, in that moment was there something about God (and about yourself) that you were failing to grasp?

15. What does it truly mean to you to walk together with Jesus, side by side?

16. In being yoked to Jesus, do you have any fear of losing your freedom?

17. At this time in your life, are you fully engaged in the work of God's kingdom?

Yoked Together

18. The yoke is *Christ's*, not yours. Why is it important to remember this?

19. What does it mean to you to be one of "God's fellow workers" (1 Corinthians 3:9)?

20. In your own work of ministry, do you labor *for* Christ, or *with* Him?

21. What true comfort and confidence do you find in knowing the Lord has you in His hand?

Choosing His Control

22. How ready and willing are you to fully accept the Lord's control in your life?

23. What is *your* "cross" that the Lord wants you to take up (Luke 14:27)? What choice must you make?

One with Christ

24. In taking upon you the yoke of Christ, what aspects of the world must you leave behind?

25. Do you find yourself thinking sometimes that the Lord's work is burdensome? If so—how does that indicate your lack of oneness with Him?

26. Do you find yourself thinking sometimes complaining about what you must do in the Lord's work? If so—how does this indicate your lack of oneness with Him?

27. In being yoked together with Christ, what does the Lord Jesus want you to *learn* from Him?

28. What exactly is the "inner invincibility" that the Lord wants you to experience?

Christ Understands This Road

29. How did Christ experience the "second mile" in His own life?

Without Complaining

30. What difference has Christ made in freeing you from a spirit of complaining?

31. What freedom from self-pity has Christ brought into your life?

The View from the Second Mile: Seeing God's Strength

32. In your own life, are you now experiencing any weariness, restlessness, or uneasiness?

33. In your own life, are you now experiencing any bitterness, disappointment, frustration, or quickness to take offense?

34. In your own life, are you now experiencing any separation from the Lord due to the influence of friends or circumstances?

35. If any of the above situations are true in your life at this time…can you hear the Lord's invitation? What does He want you to do?

36. By your coming to Him, the Lord promises you rest of soul. What does this mean to you, experientially?

Second-Mile Study

For your further reflection in God's Word—as you consider the soul rest that our Savior promises us, meditate on Hebrews 4:11–16, and find your way to the strength and help of the Lord.

AFTER YOU'VE READ CHAPTER 6—
"IN YOUR COUNTENANCE:
SEEING GOD'S JOY"

1. If you slammed your knuckles into a car's engine block, what would come out of *your* mouth?

A Concern for Joy

2. How possible is it for us to truly be *filled* with joy?

3. Take time to read through the high priestly prayer of Jesus in John 17. In these words to His Father, how do you see the Lord's concern about the *joy* of His disciples?

4. In the work of taking the gospel to a lost world, why is the *joy* of Christians so important?

5. What message does each of the following passages give us about joy?
   —John 15:5, 11
   —John 16:24
   —Romans 15:13
   —Galatians 5:22–23
   —1 John 1:4
   —Philippians 4:4

—James 1:2
—Acts 5:41

6. How does losing the joy of the Lord indicate that you're outside the Holy Spirit's control in your life?

7. Why should your salvation bring you continual joy?

His Joy Is Ours

8. How does the joy of the Lord bring an optimistic and positive outlook in your life?

9. Why does your experience of joy depend on your level of *trust* in the Lord?

Joy Comes from Trust

10. Think about the story of the disciples caught in the storm (Matthew 8:23–27). Realistically, what level of joy could they have experienced in that situation?

11. Think about Mary and Martha after their brother Lazarus died (John 11). Realistically, what level of joy could they have experienced in that situation?

12. Think about the disciples after they witnessed the crucifixion of Jesus. Realistically, what level of joy could they have experienced in that situation?

13. How do these incidents in the New Testament indicate the importance of actively trusting in the Lord's control over everything in our lives?

14. Think of a time in your own life when everything seemed out of control. Realistically, what level of joy could you have experienced in that situation?

15. Do you fully trust that God is in control of your life, and that His will for you is best?

16. What does it truly mean to be sustained by God's grace in times of difficulty, grief, and heartache?

Lighten Up

17. Have there been times in your life where you needed to "lighten up"? Do you sometimes lose sight of the privilege of serving the Lord and sharing His good news with others?

18. How well have you learned the lesson in your life that joy comes not from circumstances, but from a *relationship*?

19. Are you living "worthy of the gospel" (Philippians 1:27). Does your life demonstrate the *good* news of Christ?

From Darkness to Light

20. How well can you relate with this account of the chain-saw accident, and of experiencing the Spirit's presence and joy?

21. What does it mean personally to you to be "delivered... from the powers of darkness" and to instead have a share in "the inheritance of the saints in the light" (Colossians 1:12–13)? How do these facts influence your attitude toward life?

22. In your own Christian life, have you been guilty of being a "sourpuss"?

23. Why is a joyless Christian such a barrier to nonbelievers in receiving the gospel?

The View from the Second Mile: Seeing God's Joy

24. Why is joy more than an emotion or feeling? What really is joy?

25. What impressions do you leave on other people? When they observe your life, do they sense that the gospel is "good news"? Are you a living example that the nearness of God is your good? What do they see when they look into your eyes?

Second-Mile Study

For your further reflection in God's Word—learn more about joy in Nehemiah 8:9–12.

AFTER YOU'VE READ CHAPTER 7—
"IMPACTING THE REAL WORLD:
SEEING GOD'S HEART FOR PRAYER"

1. Why is the life of Jesus a true model and full example for your own life?

2. In what ways, if any, do you tend to resist the idea of Jesus being the model and example for everything in your life?

Prayer and Eternity

3. How keenly aware are you of the spiritual battle being waged for the souls of people around you?

4. In the last few days, how have your prayers reflected the reality of eternity?

5. Are you convinced that your greatest power for influencing the world is your ability to pray?

6. What is prayer? What does it really mean to you?

Praying as Jesus Prayed

7. Why should knowing Christ be your first priority in life?

8. What affect does sin have on our prayers?

9. When we have broken relationships with others, what affect does that have on our prayers?

10. In what way is the power of our prayer a direct measure of who we are when we're *not* praying?

Prayers That Are Heard

11. Do you desire to be a person of powerful prayer? If so, what will this require from you?

12. Are you known as a person who prays and sees the power of God move in real life circumstances? When crisis comes, do people think of you as a person they want to pray on their behalf?

Ready to Pray for Those You Love

13. What will it mean for you to go the second mile in prayer?

14. What does it mean for you to enter by prayer into the spiritual battle for the souls of lost people around you?

15. Why is a transformed prayer life the clearest evidence that a person is walking with Jesus?

A House of Prayer

16. In what ways is your church going the second mile in prayer?

17. The kind of prayer that moves heaven requires far more than many believers are prepared to give. Why are they like this?

The Loud Cries of Jesus

18. What impresses you most about the prayer life of Jesus?

19. Scripture tells us that Jesus prayed "with vehement cries and tears" (Hebrews 5:7). Do those things also characterize *your* prayer life? Are you passionate about calling out to God? Do your prayers well up from within you as a deep longing and crying out to the One who is your life?

20. What does it really mean to "cry out" to God?

The Struggle and the Victory

21. How fully do you understand that your life is a highway over which a lost world comes to the Lord?

22. How fully do you understand that in prayer you become an instrument through which God will touch the world?

23. If the salvation of your neighbors depended on your prayer life, would they stand a chance? If revival in the land depended on your prayer life, would God grant it? If judgment was coming, would your prayers stay the hand of God?

24. *Why* is the Lord calling you to pray?

The View from the Second Mile: Seeing God's Heart for Prayer

25. What can you do to seek a deeper relationship with Christ? And why is this more important than seeking a better prayer life?

Second-Mile Study

Are you going the second mile in prayer? For your further reflection in God's Word—evaluate your prayer life in light of Luke 18:1–7 and 21:36, and 1 Thessalonians 5:17.

After You've Read Chapter 8—
"Abundant Living:
Seeing God's Blessing"

1. In the way you drink, do you budget — or down it?

Satisfying Refreshment

2. When it comes to your soul's thirst, do you know how to find refreshment? Are you experiencing abundant life? Or does it seem to be just out of your reach?

3. A relationship with Christ is meant to *satisfy* (as we see in passages like John 4:14, 6:35, 7:38, 8:12, and 10:11). *Are* you satisfied? Or do you feel empty?

4. Jesus promised to give us "rivers of living water" in our heart (John 7:38). Does that statement reflect your experience at present?

Abundant Giving, Abundant Living

5. What does our experience of abundant life depend upon? What are the requirements? What is the unavoidable sacrifice that must be made?

6. "Abundant life is found in abundant living." What does that phrase mean for you?

7. Instead of waiting for abundant life, how can you *live it now?*

From Sacrifice to Blessing

8. In whatever God is calling you to do, are you truly convinced in your heart that God will be faithful as you step out in faith?

9. What have been the greatest privileges of serving others in the Lord's work that you have experienced? How did God bless your life because of it?

The Source of Abundance

10. At this time, how are you learning to...
    —love others more abundantly?
    —give more abundantly?
    —forgive more abundantly?
    —show kindness more abundantly?
    —serve the Lord with more abundant power?

11. We aren't a holding tank of blessings, but a channel. How are you sharing with others the blessings God has given you?

12. As you grow in generosity toward others, how are you experiencing God's generous heart toward you? As you give freely to others, how are you seeing God give freely to you?

13. After all God has done for you, how have you responded to Him? Is He seeing the fruit in your life that He rightfully expects to see as a result of the blessings He bestows?

A Story of Abundance

14. What stands out to you most in this account of Bob and his experiences in dealing with a critical illness?

The View from the Second Mile: Seeing God's Blessing

15. Why are God's blessings *not* "unconditional"?

16. Abundant life is experienced in direct correlation to how we live it. Do you live abundantly? Do you give to others freely and generously?

17. How well do you understand this kingdom principle: "With the measure you use, it will be measured back to you" (Matthew 7:2)?

Second-Mile Study

To deepen your experience of the abundant life promised by your Lord and Savior, reflect again on His promises in John 4:14, 6:35, 7:38, 8:12, and 10:11. Listen in these words for the Lord's specific reminder to *you*.

AFTER YOU'VE READ CHAPTER 9—
"A PARABLE OF THE SECOND MILE:
SEEING A LIFE WELL SPENT"

1. In prayer to your Creator and Lord, ask Him to lead you into the second mile—into places you've never been, and into an existence that's far beyond anything you could experience on your own.

2. What is your heart's response as your Savior asks, "Will you walk with Me on the second mile?"

3. In this moment, are you staying close enough to Jesus to take His hand and let Him lead you—close enough to recognize His voice and respond to His directions, even in the darkness?

A Time to Forgive

4. Why is full forgiveness of others necessary before you can go forward on the second mile?

5. Who do you need to forgive at this time?

A Time to Bless

6. How well do you realize the power you have to bring joy into the lives of others by your words of blessing?

7. Who do you need to bless at this time?

A Time to Do Good

8. How should we determine *who* to do good to? What is the correct basis for doing a good deed?

9. Who do you need to do good to at this time?

A Time to Give All

10. How can you fully give your life to the Lord at this time?

11. Have you allowed the Lord to take your dreams and replace them with the Father's will?

12. Have you allowed the Lord to take your human strategies for service and replace them with His kingdom ways?

13. Have you allowed the Lord to take your reputation and replace it with the glory of God?

14. Is your life no longer your own? Do you fully acknowledge that it belongs to Another?

At the Final Gate

15. As you follow the Lord on the second mile, where can you expect this to finally lead you?

The View from the Second Mile: Seeing a Life Well Spent

16. What specific opportunities do you have at this time to impact your time in eternity?

17. As eternity looms…look around you. Who is lonely and hurting? Who is buried in sin and longing to become free? Who is lost and longing for hope?

18. What are the most significant things you have learned from going through this book?